HOW YOU LIVE WITH JESUS

Catechism for Today's Young Catholic

Handbook of Basic Belief, Practices, Prayers

With Guide Notes for Teachers and Parents

A Redemptorist Pastoral Publication

LIGUORI
PUBLICATIONS

One Liguori Drive
Liguori, Missouri 63057
(314) 464-2500

Imprimi Potest:
Edmund T. Langton, C.SS.R.
Provincial, St. Louis Province
Redemptorist Fathers

Imprimatur:
+ John N. Wurm, Ph.D., S.T.D.
Vicar General, Archdiocese of St. Louis

The Imprimi Potest and Imprimatur are a declaration that a book or pamphlet is considered to be free from doctrinal or moral error. It is not implied that those who have granted the Imprimi Potest and Imprimatur agree with the contents, opinions or statements expressed.

Copyright © 1981, Liguori Publications
ISBN 0-89243-137-7
Library of Congress Catalog Card Number: 81-80097
Printed in U.S.A.

Text by Roger Marchand
Catechetical advisers:
Christopher Farrell, C.SS.R.,
JoAnn Ebert, Monica Marchand,
and Terri Van Diver
Cover and internal design by
Pam Hummelsheim and Roger Marchand
Illustrations by Jim Corbett
Editorial services by Martha Perry

Excerpts from SHARING THE LIGHT OF FAITH, National Catechetical Directory for Catholics of the United States, copyright © 1979, by the United States Catholic Conference, Department of Education, Washington, D.C., are used by permission of copyright owner. All rights reserved.

Excerpts from THE JERUSALEM BIBLE, copyright © 1966 by Darton, Longman & Todd, Ltd. and Doubleday & Company, Inc. Used by permission of the publisher.

Quotations from The Documents of Vatican II, Abbott-Gallagher edition were reprinted with permission of America Press, Inc., 106 W. 56 Street, New York, New York 10019. Copyright © 1966. All rights reserved.

Scripture text is from the *Good News Bible* - New Testament: Copyright © American Bible Society 1966, 1971, 1976. Used by permission.

Contents

Dear Parent and Teacher 7

UNIT ONE: YOU ARE A CHILD OF GOD

1. Where did the world come from? (God; Creation; Person) 9
2. What makes you wonderful? (Person; Free will; Soul) 10
3. Why did God create you? (The Father; Heaven) 11

Workshop 12

UNIT TWO: GOD PROMISED A COVENANT FAMILY

4. What was God's earliest promise? (Covenant) 13
5. What did God promise Abraham and Sarah? (Family; Covenant) 14
6. What did God promise Moses and the people? (Covenant) 15
7. What are the Ten Words of the Covenant? (Ten Commandments) 16
8. What did God promise about King David? (King; Messiah) 17
9. What did God promise through the prophets? (New Covenant) 18

Workshop 19

UNIT THREE: GOD GIVES YOU JESUS

10. How was Jesus born? (Annunciation; Birth of Jesus) 21
11. What happened when Jesus was twelve? (Finding in the Temple) 22
12. What does Jesus teach about God? (Abba; Mercy; Love) 23
13. What does Jesus teach about people? (Love; Matthew 25) 24
14. How does Jesus treat "forgotten" people? (Mercy; Forgiveness) 25
15. What does Jesus teach about praying? (The Our Father) 26
16. What happened at Jesus' Last Supper? (Eucharist) 27
17. How and why did Jesus die? (Trial; Crucifixion) 28
18. What happened when Jesus rose? (Risen Lord; Eucharist) 29

Workshop 30

UNIT FOUR: YOU LIVE IN THE SPIRIT OF JESUS

19. When did the Father send the Holy Spirit? (Pentecost) 33
20. How does the Spirit live in you? (Grace; Faith; Hope; Love) 34
21. What seven helps does the Spirit give you? (Gifts of the Spirit) . 35
22. Why are you one of God's family? (Trinity) 36

Workshop 37

UNIT FIVE: YOU LIVE IN THE CHURCH OF JESUS

23. Who makes the Church the Body of Jesus? (RISEN JESUS) 39
24. Who makes your family "the Church"? (JESUS; FAMILY) 40
25. Who makes your parish a family? (JESUS IN THE EUCHARIST) 41
26. What do One, Holy, Catholic, Apostolic mean?(MARKS OF CHURCH) 42
Workshop 43

UNIT SIX: YOU MEET JESUS IN BIBLE, PRAYER

27. What is the Bible? (OLD AND NEW TESTAMENTS; INSPIRED WORD) 45
28. How do you pray with the Bible? (READING, PRAYING THE BIBLE) 46
29. What are the mysteries of the Rosary? (SUMMARY OF THE GOSPEL) 47
30. How do you pray the Rosary? (THE FIVE-DECADE ROSARY) 48
31. How do you pray mini-prayers? (PRAYERS FROM THE BIBLE) 49
32. How can you learn to live the Good News? (EVANGELIZATION) 50
Workshop 51

UNIT SEVEN: YOU MEET JESUS IN LITURGY

33. What is a sacrament? (SIGN; MEETING WITH JESUS; GRACE) 53
34. How do sacraments help you? (HELPS ON THE JOURNEY OF LIFE) 54
35. How does Baptism change you? (NEW BIRTH; LIFE IN THE CHURCH) 55
36. How does Confirmation change you? (SPIRIT;GROWTH) 56
37. How does the Eucharist change you? (BREAD; BODY; LIFE) 57
38. How does Reconciliation change you? (PENANCE; ABSOLUTION) 58
39. How do you celebrate Reconciliation? (THE RITE OF PENANCE) 59
40. Who should be anointed? (SICKNESS; HEALING; GETTING READY) 60
41. How is marriage a covenant? (PERMANENT, EXCLUSIVE SHARING) 61
42. Why do people become priests? (HOLY ORDERS; ROLE OF CLERGY) 62
43. What are the parts of the Mass? (LITURGY OF WORD, EUCHARIST) 63
44. How can Sunday Mass help your family? (FAMILY AT EUCHARIST) 69
Workshop 70

UNIT EIGHT: YOU LIVE BY JESUS' LAW OF LOVE

45. Why do people suffer? (ORIGINAL, PERSONAL SIN; SALVATION) 73
46. What is a personal sin? (TYPES, CONDITIONS FOR PERSONAL SIN) 74
47. How do you die to sin? (CONVERSION; FAMILY; RECONCILIATION) 75
48. How does God ask you to love? (CONSCIENCE; DECISION-MAKING) 76
49. When is your conscience Christian? (THE BEATITUDES) 77
50. What are some signs of a true Christian? (WORKS OF MERCY) 81
51. What Catholic duties help you to love? (PRECEPTS OF THE CHURCH) 82
Workshop 83

UNIT NINE: YOU LIVE WITH MARY AND THE SAINTS

52. What should you know about Mary? (MARIAN TEACHING) 85
53. How can you show Mary you love her? (PRAYERS TO MARY) 86
54. Who is a saint? (SAINTS; COMMUNION OF SAINTS) 87
Workshop 88

UNIT TEN: HOME IS WITH GOD

55. What happens when you die? (JUDGMENT; FINAL DESTINY) 89
56. What will heaven be like? (HAPPINESS; JOY; HOME AT LAST) 90
57. What will happen when Jesus returns? (JUDGMENT; NEW EARTH) 91
Workshop 92

Appendix A: Important Catholic Prayers 93
**Appendix B: An Examination of Conscience Based on
the Commandments and the Words of Jesus** 94

Dear Parent and Teacher . . .

This Handbook is written mainly for young Catholics in the middle years of elementary school. This Handbook can also be used by Catholics in various other situations — for example, those who need a survey or a review of Catholic belief and practice.

Catholic School and CCD/PSR Teachers

If you teach several religion periods a week in a Catholic school, we recommend that you use the Leader's Guide for this Handbook. If you are a weekly CCD or PSR teacher, we recommend the Leader's Guide to you, too. You do not absolutely need the Leader's Guide to use this Handbook in class. But you will find it a great help. The Leader's Guide develops the all-important experiential dimension. It is a bridge between doctrinal content and real life.

Parents Using This Handbook

Parents, we recommend that you use this Handbook with your child *without* the Leader's Guide. You can certainly benefit from using the Leader's Guide. But this Handbook has many built-in guide features for you — and for classroom teachers too. In that sense, this Handbook is self-contained.

A Self-contained Text

One of the guide features in this Handbook are the notes in small print. Look, for example, on page 9. Whether you are in a classroom or at home, these notes will point you to stories, examples, and backup materials.

The *Workshop* Sections

Every Unit in this Handbook concludes with a section called *Workshop*. Look, for example, on page 12. Each *Workshop* has four parts: Words to Know; Mini-test; Write and Share at Home; Pray and Do. Use each *Workshop* section first as an aid to class preparation. Then use it with your child(ren) after you have gone through the Unit together.

Words to Know

The words in this part of each *Workshop* ought to be familiar to every Catholic, even the young. Most of the descriptions, definitions, and information you find here are written on an adult level. Select those points and ideas that your child(ren) can grasp. When you are focusing on a word, refer back to the page on which it is used in the text.

Mini-test

The questions in this part of each *Workshop* focus on material in that Unit. Answers to the questions are on the pages indicated at the end of each question. These questions are cognitive-content questions. In a general way, they cover all of the content in the Unit. Teachers, you will probably want to use most or all of these questions, plus other questions of your own that you judge to be important. Parents, you may want to select certain questions that you judge to be especially important.

Write and Share at Home

The material in this part does its best work in a family setting. The questions get into personal feelings, attitudes, and values. Parents, this material offers a great opportunity for you to show your child(ren) your own deep faith, hope, and love. No one has a deeper influence on your children's religious future than you. Teachers, do not let the phrase "at Home" keep you out of the Write and Share material. Your class is a faith community in which personal attitudes need to be shared.

Pray and Do

Knowing the Good News of Jesus is only a beginning. The News is really Good only when we *live* and *share* it. Use this Pray and Do material as a springboard. Develop prayers and projects of your own. The material in this Handbook is valuable only to the extent that you use it to grow *together* in faith, hope, and love of Jesus and His Body — your family, your class, your fellow parishioners. Parents and teachers, remember the words of the noted English priest-educator, Canon Drinkwater:

You educate to some extent . . . by what you say, more by what you do, and still more by what you are; but most of all by the things you love.

— The Redemptorist Pastoral Team

UNIT ONE: YOU ARE A CHILD OF GOD

1 Where did the world come from? (God; Creation; Person)

Billions of years ago, scientists say, there was an explosion called the Big Bang. Before the Big Bang, our world was not here. After the Big Bang, an ocean of hot gases and atoms were left from the blast. At great speed, the gases traveled away from the spot. As they traveled, great globs of gas turned into huge balls of hot light. You can see these balls of light when you look up in the sky at night. They are the stars.

Before the Big Bang, our world was not here. There was nothing here at all. And then — BANG! — a whole world came into being. You have to wonder: WHO caused the Big Bang?

Read Genesis 1:1-23 – the first five days of creation.

Read Genesis 1:26-29 – the creation of humankind.

Read about the Big Bang in an elementary science text.

The very first words in the Bible tell us: the world was created by GOD! *In the beginning GOD created the heavens and the earth. (Genesis 1:1).* GOD created everything: stars, sun and moon. As time passed, there appeared mountains, rivers, and every kind of animal.

GOD created everything. But there is a very special part of His creation that GOD loves best. That part is called *human beings*. The creation that GOD loves best is *you!*

As a human person you are *sacred* or *holy*. You can think of GOD. You can even talk to GOD. You can do these amazing things because GOD created you "in the image of himself." (Genesis 1:27) You are *sacred* because, some day, you will go home to GOD. You are the greatest because GOD is the GREATEST.

9

2 What makes you wonderful?
(Person; Free will; Soul)

At the moment you began living, you were a tiny cell in your mother's body. At that same moment, somewhere, a baby pup began living in its mother. The pup was born. He grew into a big dog. But he never learned to talk. He has never read a book. Some day, the dog might wander into church. If he does, will he pray while he is in there? No. Dogs never pray.

Like your friend the dog, you have two eyes, a mouth, most of the same bodily parts. Does this mean you are just a smarter kind of animal? No. You are much more wonderful than that. You are a *person*.

Suppose you were hungry and someone put a delicious hamburger in front of you. As hungry as you were, you could still say, "Give this hamburger to someone who needs it more than I do." Now, put that hamburger before your big, hungry dog. Can he keep from eating it? No, he cannot — because he has no *free will*. You do have free will. You can say yes to the hamburger or no to the hamburger. You are a *person*.

Read Genesis 1:27 and 28 – human uniqueness.

Give, and ask for, other examples of free will.

In the Bible, spirit = a person's life force which returns to God at death.

Like the animals, you have a wonderful body. But your *soul*, or *spirit*, makes you even more wonderful. When you die, your soul will go out of your body. Your body will die. But you — your soul — will go on living forever. Your *soul* is what makes you really wonderful.

10

3 Why did God create you?
(The Father; Heaven)

Do you remember the story of the prodigal son who left home? This young man thought he would be happy away from his father. But that was a mistake. He turned out to be very unhappy.

So the young man decided to go back home. He thought his father would be angry with him when they came face-to-face. But when his father saw him, the father hugged and kissed him. It was then that the young man discovered the truth: *My father really loves me!* From then on, the father and son lived together, happy forever. (Luke 15:11-32)

Read about Pinocchio, a boy who left home and returned.

Find parallels in The Wizard of Oz, Cinderella, The Ugly Duckling, Snow White, Sleeping Beauty.

That story is your story. The Father in your story is God. The person who is discovering the truth is you. The truth is: *God, your Father, loves you with His whole heart*. He created you because He loves you. When you love someone, you want the person to be with you. That is how God feels about you.

Read John 14:1-3 – Jesus is preparing a place for us.

God wants you to live with Him. After your life on earth, you will go home to be with your Father in heaven. That is why He created you.

11

Workshop

Words to Know
- ATOMS: the very tiny particles that all physical things are made of.
- BODY: the physical part of you that sees, hears, touches; the physical part of you that others see, hear, touch.
- GOD: the One who created the world, including you.
- CREATE: to make out of nothing.
- CREATION: the whole world and everything in it.
- PERSON: the whole you, body and soul.
- SOUL, SPIRIT: the real "you" who thinks and loves; the part of you that will keep on living after your body dies.
- SACRED, HOLY: persons and things that are very special because they are close to God.
- HEAVEN: being very happy with God.

Mini-test
1. Where did the world come from? (Page 9)
2. What is there about you that is like the animals? (Page 10)
3. What makes you wonderful? (Page 10)
4. Why did God create you? (Page 11)

Write and Share at Home
1. With one or more of your relatives, make up a "List of Wonders" that show how great God is. Here is a start: the Big Bang; Niagara Falls; a little baby; a person smiling . . . .
2. Everybody write down what you like about the story of the son and his father on page 11. Then take turns reading to each other what you wrote.

Pray and Do
1. Memorize this line from the Psalms:
   O LORD, our LORD, how great is your name over all the earth!
2. Read the first account of creation in Genesis, chapter 1.
3. Read the story of the son who left home in the Gospel of Saint Luke, chapter 15.

UNIT TWO: GOD PROMISED A COVENANT FAMILY

4 What was God's earliest promise? (Covenant)

Genesis, the first book in the Bible, starts out with good news! In chapter 1 of Genesis, God creates the world. Everything God creates is wonderful. Especially wonderful are the people — God creates them "in the image of himself." (Genesis 1:27) God has a wise plan for His people. If they live by God's plan, their world will be a garden of happiness. The future looks bright indeed.

But then bad news enters the picture. In chapter 3 of Genesis, Adam and Eve, the man and woman, commit the original sin. They go against God's plan for them. Now they feel afraid of God. They are no longer happy. Soon other people commit sins. In chapter 4, jealous Cain murders his own brother, Abel. By chapter 11, people have become very proud and foolish. They say, "Let us make a name for ourselves" and they try to build a tower all the way up to heaven. God stops the proud fools. He causes them to speak different languages. Now they cannot even understand one another. Because of sin, the world has gotten into very deep trouble.

But all is not lost! God always loves the people He created "in the image of himself." He promises a "lasting Covenant." The happy day will come, God says, when people will again live together with Me. (Genesis 9:12-16) Trust Me, God says. The news is good. I promise.

"This is the sign of the Covenant..."

Read Genesis 4:1-12 – the story of Cain and Abel.

Read Genesis 6:9-8:22 – Noah and the Ark.

Read Genesis 11:1-9 – the Tower of Babel.

5 What did God promise Abraham and Sarah?
(Family; Covenant)

There once was a man named Abram. God knew that Abram was a good man. God spoke to him and said: "Leave your country for a new land I will show you. *I will make your family a great people.*" Abram did not know what to think. Where would God lead him? Traveling was dangerous — would God protect Abram's family? Abram decided he would trust God. He and his wife Sarai left their home in Mesopotamia. They began their journey of faith. They traveled to a land called Canaan.

Many years later, Abram was a very old man in Canaan. God said to Abram: "From now on you will be called Abraham. Your wife Sarai will be called Sarah. Sarah is too old to have children. But she will bear a son named Isaac. With Isaac I will start my Covenant."

Isaac was born, just as God had promised. After he grew up, Isaac married Rebecca. Rebecca gave birth to twin boys, Esau and Jacob. It was Jacob — also called Israel — who became the father of the people of Israel.

When people in the Bible get new names, it means they have an important mission from God. Abraham and Sarah are very important. They trusted God by making a long, dangerous journey. Your life is a journey of faith. You need to trust God. Ask Abraham and Sarah to help you. With faith like theirs, you help others to have faith in God.

Read Genesis 12:1-9 – God's promise to Abram.

Read Genesis 17:1-8,15-20 – new names for Abraham and Sarah, and the promise of a Covenant with Isaac.

Read Genesis 28:10-19 – Jacob's dream and God's promise.

Read Romans 4:18 – words of Saint Paul about Abraham.

6 What did God promise Moses and the people? (Covenant)

Jacob had twelve sons. Joseph, one of the sons, became an important man in Egypt. But then Egypt got a new king. This king turned Jacob's sons and their families into slaves. They were called Hebrews.

Four hundred years later the Hebrews were still slaves. But now God gave them a great leader named Moses. One day Moses saw a burning bush. From the bush he heard the voice of God saying, "Moses, Moses." God told him to go to the king and say: "Let my people go free." Moses obeyed. He went to the palace and told Pharaoh (the king) what God wanted. Pharaoh replied: "I will not free the Hebrew people."

God now sent ten plagues upon Egypt. The tenth, final plague was so terrible that Pharaoh finally told Moses: "Take your people and leave at once." The Hebrew families had eaten a special meal called the Passover meal. They were now ready to travel. When Moses gave the word, the Hebrews began their journey — the great escape, or Exodus, from Egypt.

Read Exodus 14:5-31 – the crossing of the sea.

Read Exodus 16 and 17:1-7 – manna, quail, and water.

Read Exodus 19:16-25 – God appears on Sinai.

Read Exodus 1:8-22 and 2:1-10 – the Hebrews in slavery, and Moses as a baby.

Read Exodus 3:1-12 – God calls Moses.

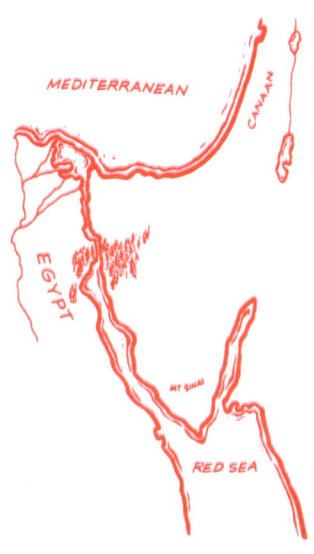

The Hebrews traveled through the desert. They needed food and water. God gave them manna, a bread they found in the desert every morning. They finally came to the wilderness of Sinai. Here God called Moses up to the mountaintop. God made this promise: *"If you obey My voice and keep My Covenant, you will be My very own people."* God also said: *"I am the Lord God who brought you out of Egypt, the land of slavery."* Then God spoke the Ten Words — the Commandments of the Covenant. And He gave the people this promise about the land of Canaan: *"You will inherit the land."*

7 What are the Ten Words of the Covenant? (The Ten Commandments)

Here are the Ten Words that God gave to Moses at Mount Sinai. They are called *the Ten Commandments.* It was very important for Israel to keep these Commandments. Keeping the Commandments was Israel's way of being God's people. It was their way of being faithful to the Covenant.

1. *I am Yahweh your God who brought you out of the land of Egypt, out of the house of slavery.*
YOU SHALL HAVE NO GODS EXCEPT ME.
(Exodus 20:2; Deuteronomy 5:6-7)

2. YOU SHALL NOT UTTER THE NAME OF YAHWEH YOUR GOD TO MISUSE IT.
(Exodus 20:7; Deuteronomy 5:11)

3. OBSERVE THE SABBATH DAY AND KEEP IT HOLY.
(Deuteronomy 5:12)

4. HONOR YOUR FATHER AND YOUR MOTHER.
(Exodus 20:12; Deuteronomy 5:16)

5. YOU SHALL NOT KILL.
(Exodus 20:13; Deuteronomy 5:17)

6. YOU SHALL NOT COMMIT ADULTERY.
(Exodus 20:14; Deuteronomy 5:18)

7. YOU SHALL NOT STEAL.
(Exodus 20:15; Deuteronomy 5:19)

8. YOU SHALL NOT BEAR FALSE WITNESS AGAINST YOUR NEIGHBOR.
(Exodus 20:16; Deuteronomy 5:20)

9. YOU SHALL NOT COVET YOUR NEIGHBOR'S WIFE.
(Deuteronomy 5:21)

10. YOU SHALL NOT SET YOUR HEART ON . . . ANYTHING THAT IS HIS.
(Deuteronomy 5:21)

*This is what the Lord asks of you, only this:
to act justly, to love tenderly,
and to walk humbly with your God.*

Micah 6:8

8 What did God promise about King David?
(King; Messiah)

The people of Israel did "inherit the land." After Moses died, their army captured Jericho and other cities in Canaan. But the people kept forgetting God. They would break the sacred Covenant by worshiping Canaanite gods. When this happened, God would let Canaanite armies nearly destroy them. The Israelites would turn back to God. God would then raise up a military leader, called a Judge, to rescue the people.

After 200 years of fighting against their enemies, some Israelite leaders said: "Let us become stronger by uniting under a king." Others said, "No, God is our only king." Finally the people shouted: "GIVE US A KING!" The prophet Samuel gave in to this demand. He anointed Saul with oil, making him Israel's first king.

When Saul died, young David from Bethlehem became king. David captured a town called Jerusalem and made it his fortress. King Solomon, David's son, built the first Temple there. Israel was now a mighty kingdom with a great Temple, the house of God.

God had kept His promise about the land. Now God promised that He Himself would dwell forever in David's "house" and "kingdom." (2 Samuel, chapter 7) One thousand years later, this Covenant promise came true: God sent His chosen Messiah, Jesus Christ, Son of David.

Read Joshua 6 – the walls of Jericho fall down.

Read 2 Samuel 5:1-12 – David becomes king, captures Jerusalem.

Read 1 Kings 6:1-14, 8:1-9 – the Temple and the Ark of the Covenant.

A Psalm of David

O Lord, You are my lamp.
You light up my darkness.
You are my strength, my power.
You set me free
   because You love me.
I will give You thanks, Lord.
I will sing Your praise forever.

Adapted from 2 Samuel 22

9 What did God promise through the prophets? (New Covenant)

God picked certain people in Israel to be prophets. A prophet's job was to speak out and remind Israel of the Covenant. Some prophets predicted important future events. Here are two prophets and some things they said.

I am JEREMIAH. God called me to be a prophet six hundred and twenty-six years before Christ. My job was to tell Israel bad news. I warned: "Many of you people with money and power are cruel, especially to the poor. You go to Temple and worship. But that is a big show; your hearts are not with God. So God is going to let an enemy from the north come and destroy you!" People called me a traitor for saying that. They beat me up. I was sad for Israel, but my final word was full of hope. Through me, God predicted: "The days are coming when I will make a *new covenant* with Israel."

I am the prophet known as SECOND ISAIAH. 587 years before Christ, the armies of Babylon destroyed Jerusalem and the Temple (just as Jeremiah had warned). Most of the people were taken to Babylon as prisoners. About 45 years later, I announced that King Cyrus of Persia would conquer Babylon and let the Israelites return home. This came true in the year 538. I also foresaw a mysterious "Servant of the Lord" whose suffering would save God's people. To see who this Servant reminds you of, read Isaiah 42:1-4, 49:1-7, 50:4-11, and 52:13 to 53:12.

Read Jeremiah 31:31-34 – the New Covenant.

Read Jonah 1 and 2 – Jonah and the whale.

Workshop

Words to Know

- MESOPOTAMIA: the land between the Tigris and Euphrates rivers; modern Iraq. It is roughly 400 miles northeast of Canaan.
- COVENANT: the agreement between God and His people, Israel. God loves and takes care of His people. They return God's love by being faithful to His word.
- PLAGUES: epidemics and other disasters.
- PASSOVER: the night the lives of the Hebrews' first-born children were spared, or passed over, by God; the yearly Jewish feast that is celebrated by a meal.
- EXODUS: all the things God did to free the Hebrews from slavery in Egypt; the acts of God in Exodus, chapters 1 through 15.
- CANAAN: the land, between Syria and Egypt, which God gave to the Israelites.
- JUDGES: military leaders who conquered enemies of Israel.
- BETHLEHEM: a town five miles south of Jerusalem. It was the birthplace of David, and the place where Samuel anointed David king of Israel.
- JERUSALEM: the city in central Palestine which David captured and made his capitol. The city is also called Zion, the name of the hill on which the Temple was built.
- TEMPLE: Israel's great house of God in Jerusalem. In the center of the Temple was the "Holy of Holies" where God was present in a special way.
- MESSIAH: a king, from the family of David, who will save the world; Jesus Christ.
- PROPHET: a person God chooses to speak His word in public and demand justice for the people.
- SERVANT OF THE LORD: a mysterious figure whose suffering and death will save God's people. Foreseen in the Book of Isaiah, the Servant is Jesus; see Matthew 12:15-21 and Isaiah 42:1-4.

Mini-test
1. What good news did God promise in chapter 9 of Genesis? (Page 13)
2. What did Abraham and Sarah do that shows they trusted God completely? (Page 14)
3. What great promise did God make to Abraham and Sarah? (Page 14)
4. What was the Covenant agreement that God made with the Hebrew people at Mount Sinai? (Page 15)
5. Recite the Ten Commandments. (Page 16)
6. What was King David's birthplace? What makes it important? (Page 17)
7. What great promise did God make about David's house and kingdom? How did God keep that promise? (Page 17)
8. What famous prophecy did God make through Jeremiah? (Page 18)
9. On pages 13 through 18 of this book, how many important promises does God make and keep? Count them.

Write and Share at Home
1. Pages 14 and 15 of this book give part of the family tree of Israel. Draw it on a sheet of paper.
2. The Hebrew families lived a hard life in Egypt for over 400 years. Think of hard times your parents or grandparents have lived through. Share these memories.

Pray and Do
1. Read the stories of Abraham, Isaac, Jacob, Moses, and King David in the Books of Genesis, Exodus, 1 and 2 Samuel. (One of the best children's Bibles available is A CHILD'S BIBLE — two color-illustrated paperbacks covering the Old and New Testaments. Published by Pan Books Ltd in Great Britain, A CHILD'S BIBLE is available in the United States from Paulist Press.)
2. The Bible is filled with promises that God has made, and kept, out of love for His people. What promise can you make that will help your family to be happier? On a piece of paper, write: *I promise* . . . . Do not tell anyone what your promise is. Just keep it.

UNIT THREE: GOD GIVES YOU JESUS

10 How was Jesus born? (Annunciation; Birth of Jesus)

One thousand years after King David lived, a young lady named Mary was working at home in the town of Nazareth. Suddenly God's angel, Gabriel, came into the room she was in. Gabriel said: "Greetings, Mary. God loves you very much. You are to have a son named Jesus, who will be king of Israel." Mary was surprised. She asked: "How will this happen?" The angel told Mary that the Holy Spirit of God would make it happen. Mary said: "I belong to the Lord. Let it be done."

Joseph, Mary's husband-to-be, soon learned that she was to have a baby. He was surprised. But in a dream, an angel said to him: "Joseph, this is the work of the Holy Spirit. Mary's child will be the Savior. Marry her."

Read Luke 1:5-25 – the Birth of John.

Read Luke 1:26-38 – the Annunciation.

Read Luke 1:39-45 – the Visitation.

Read Luke 2:1-20 – the Birth of Jesus, the shepherds.

Read Luke 2:22-38 – the Presentation.

Read Matthew 2:1-12 – the visit of the Wise Men.

Read Matthew 2:13-23 – the flight to Egypt.

Months later, Mary and Joseph journeyed to Bethlehem, the city of David, to register for the census. They went there because Joseph belonged to the family tree of King David. Now came the time for Jesus to be born. Mary and Joseph needed a place to stay. But the only place they could find was a stable for sheep and cows. That is where the Virgin Mary had her baby. Jesus, the Son of God, the Savior of the world, was born in a stable in Bethlehem.

11 What happened when Jesus was twelve? (Finding in the Temple)

When Jesus was twelve years old, Mary and Joseph took Him on a trip to Jerusalem. It was Passover, the time of year when Jewish people thank God for the Exodus from Egypt.

When it came time to go home, Mary and Joseph thought Jesus was with His aunts and uncles. They left Jerusalem without Him. But the next day, Mary and Joseph discovered that no one knew where Jesus was. Very worried, Mary and Joseph hurried back to Jerusalem.

Read Luke 2:41-52 – the Finding in the Temple.

After three days of searching, Mary and Joseph finally found Jesus. He was in the Temple, sitting with priests and teachers. These people were discussing important matters. Jesus was telling them things that made them wonder: How can a twelve-year-old child know so much?

While this was going on, Mary and Joseph walked up to Jesus. Mary said, "Son, why have you done this to us?" Jesus said: "Why did you have to look for me? Didn't you know that I had to be in my Father's house?" Mary did not know what to say to Jesus. But she knew this: When Jesus said "my Father," He meant GOD.

After that, "Jesus went back with them to Nazareth, where he was obedient to them. His mother treasured all these things in her heart." (Luke 2:41-52)

Read Matthew 3:13-17 – Jesus is baptized by John.

Read Matthew 4:12-17 – Jesus begins His work.

Read Luke 5:1-11 – Jesus calls His first disciples.

Read John 2:1-10 – Jesus changes water into wine.

12 What does Jesus teach about God?
(*Abba;* Mercy; Love)

The Jewish people had great reverence for God. In public, they would not even say His name. But Jesus was different — He talked about God everywhere He went. He even had a special name for God — *ABBA* — "dearest Dad."

The Jewish people thought of God as Yahweh, the mighty Lord of Mount Sinai. Some people thought of Yahweh as a strict judge who likes to punish sinners. Jesus helped His followers to see that God is our loving, forgiving Father.

One time, a group of people who were very strict complained about Jesus. They said that He was too full of love for poor people and sinners. They said: "This man welcomes outcasts (people nobody likes) and even eats with them." To show that God loves outcasts, Jesus told three stories. In the first story, God is like a shepherd who leaves ninety-nine sheep to seek one sheep that is lost. When he finds the lost sheep, the shepherd is filled with joy. In the second story, a woman finds a valuable coin she had lost. So the woman throws a big party to celebrate. Jesus remarks: "In the same way, I tell you, the angels of God rejoice over one sinner who repents." The third story is about the son who left home. When the son goes back home, his father hugs and kisses him. (Luke, chapter 15)

God is your *Abba*, your dearest Father. He is with you, loving you at every moment. The Spirit of Jesus lives in your heart. Within you, the Spirit cries out, "Father, my Father." (Galatians 4:6)

Read Matthew 6:25-34 – *God takes care of us.*

Read John 14:1-7 – *your home is with the Father.*

Read Matthew 18:1-4 – *children are the greatest.*

13 What does Jesus teach about people? (Love; Matthew 25)

Jesus taught the people how to love God, our Father. Jesus taught the people how to be happy. One day a man in the crowd asked Jesus: "Teacher, which is the greatest commandment in the Law?" In reply, Jesus gave two great Commandments of Love:

"YOU MUST LOVE THE LORD YOUR GOD WITH ALL YOUR HEART, WITH ALL YOUR SOUL, AND WITH ALL YOUR MIND. THIS IS THE GREATEST AND MOST IMPORTANT COMMANDMENT. THE SECOND MOST IMPORTANT COMMANDMENT IS LIKE IT: YOU MUST LOVE YOUR FELLOWMAN AS YOURSELF." (Matthew 22:37-39)

Jesus said that whenever you help anyone, you are really helping Jesus Himself! Saint Matthew's Gospel tells about Jesus as King at the end of the world. People who helped others during life ask the King: *"When, Lord, did we ever see you hungry and feed you, or thirsty and give you drink? . . . When did we ever see you sick or in prison, and visit you?"* Never forget Jesus' answer to those questions. He says:

"WHENEVER YOU DID THIS FOR ONE OF THE LEAST IMPORTANT OF THESE BROTHERS OF MINE, YOU DID IT FOR ME!" (Matthew 25:37-40)

When you help others, you are loving Jesus Himself.

Read Matthew 5:43-48 – Love your enemies.

Read Matthew 7:12 – the Golden Rule.

14 How does Jesus treat "forgotten" people? (Mercy; Forgiveness)

Today, where you live, there are "forgotten" people around you. Some are *old people* who live alone. They have no one to help them. They are afraid of falling down or getting mugged. They are very lonely. Many *sick people* are "forgotten." They cannot get out to see friends and have fun. They are very lonely. You can help them.

Jesus loves "forgotten" people. The worse off they are, the more He feels for them. He cured people who were crippled and blind. He hugged them and made them feel loved. (Luke 13:10-13; John 9:1-7)

Jesus even made friends with sinners who were hated by the people. Zacchaeus, the rich tax collector, was a crook. He cheated people out of their money. But after Jesus was kind to him, Zacchaeus became an honest man. Zacchaeus knew Jesus loved him. That helped Zacchaeus to love others. (Luke 19:1-10) No matter what they have done wrong, Jesus always forgives people who want to be forgiven.

Read Luke 5:27-32 – Jesus ate with sinners.

Jesus has a *special love* for "forgotten" people — the old, the sick, the poor — *people who have no one to love them.* When you show real love for these people, you are loving Jesus Himself. When you forgive and show mercy, you help people to know Jesus.

Read Luke 7:11-17 (esp. verse 13) – Jesus felt sorry for suffering people.

15 What does Jesus teach about praying? (The Our Father)

When you love someone, you want to talk to him or her. When you love God, you talk to Him. This is called praying.

During His life on earth, Jesus was very close to His Father. Jesus was busy every day. But He always took time out to talk to His Father. Saint Luke says: "he would go away to lonely places, where he prayed." (Luke 5:16)

Whenever He made a big decision, Jesus would always pray. Choosing twelve of His disciples to be special Apostles was a very big decision. Before He chose them, Jesus prayed all night. Saint Luke says that He "spent the whole night there praying to God. When day came he called his disciples to him and chose twelve of them, whom he named apostles . . . ." (Luke 6:12-13)

Read Luke 3:21-22 – Jesus was praying when the Father spoke to Him.

Read Luke 9:28-36 – Jesus was praying when He was transfigured.

Read Luke 22:39-46 – Jesus prayed to accept the Father's will.

Every day the disciples saw Jesus go off alone to pray. They wondered: What does Jesus say to the Father? One day, when He finished praying, a disciple said to Jesus: "Lord, teach us to pray." Jesus said: "This is how you should pray." Then He taught them the Our Father.

Our Father, who art in heaven, hallowed be thy name; thy kingdom come; thy will be done on earth as it is in heaven. Give us this day our daily bread; and forgive us our trespasses as we forgive those who trespass against us; and lead us not into temptation, but deliver us from evil.

16 What happened at Jesus' Last Supper? (Eucharist)

The day before Jesus died is called Holy Thursday. That Thursday night, Jesus had His Last Supper with His Apostles. He told them: "I have wanted so much to eat this Passover with you before I suffer!" (Luke 22:15)

Before the meal, Jesus washed and dried the Apostles' feet. Then He said: "I have set an example for you." (John 13:15) He loved His friends so much that He wanted to be their Servant. He wanted them to love others in the same way.

After saying grace, Jesus broke some bread and gave a piece to each Apostle. He said: *"This is my body which is given for you. Do this in memory of me."* Jesus then passed the cup of wine to each Apostle. He said: *"This cup is God's new covenant sealed with my blood which is poured out for you."* (Luke 22:19, 20)

This Supper was the first Holy Eucharist. Jesus' friends ate the bread, His body. This made them very close to Him. The next day Jesus would shed His blood on the Cross, showing that God had begun the new Covenant with His people.

Read Luke 22:1-6, 21-23 — Judas betrays Jesus.

Every Sunday Catholics share the Holy Eucharist, Jesus' Passover meal. At the Eucharist Catholics remember the Last Supper and Jesus' sacrifice on the Cross. In the days of the Exodus, God gave bread called manna to the Hebrews in the desert. At the Eucharist God gives new "bread from heaven," the body and blood of the Risen Jesus. The Holy Eucharist is Jesus' special way of being with His friends. It is His way of helping Catholics to be His new Covenant people.

Read Mark 14:26-31 — Jesus predicts Peter's denial.

17 How and why did Jesus die? (Trial; Crucifixion)

After the Last Supper, Jesus led the Apostles to a garden called Gethsemane. He went there to pray because He knew He was going to die. Late at night when Jesus finished praying, some soldiers and guards came. They arrested Jesus. When they saw the soldiers, the Apostles were afraid and ran away.

Jesus was taken to the house of Caiaphas, the High Priest. There the Council put Jesus on trial. The High Priest questioned Him: "Are you the Messiah, the Son of the Blessed God?" "I AM," replied Jesus. When they heard that, the whole Council voted: GUILTY! He should be put to death!

The next morning they took Jesus to Pontius Pilate, the Roman governor. A crowd gathered outside Pilate's palace. Inside, Pilate questioned Jesus: "Are you the king of the Jews?" *My kingdom does not belong to this world,* Jesus said. (John 18:36) Pilate then went outside and said to the crowd: "I cannot find any reason to condemn him." But the chief priests and the guards shouted: "NAIL HIM TO THE CROSS!" Pilate feared these men. He handed Jesus over to them.

The place for crucifixion was a hill called Golgotha or Calvary. There, soldiers nailed Jesus to the Cross. They also crucified two criminals, one on each side of Him. On that Good Friday, the sun stopped shining about noon. The sky stayed dark until 3 o'clock, when Jesus cried out: *"Father! In your hands I place my spirit!"* Then He died.

Read Mark 14:43-52 – the arrest of Jesus.

Read Mark 14:53-65 – the trial before the Jewish Council.

Read Mark 14:66-72 – Peter denies Jesus.

Read Mark 15:1-15 – the trial before the Roman governor.

Read Mark 15:21-32 – the way of the cross and crucifixion.

Read Mark 15:33-47 – the death and burial of Jesus.

18 What happened when Jesus rose? (Risen Lord; Eucharist)

Now that Jesus was dead, an old friend named Joseph of Arimathaea prepared His body for burial. He put the body in a tomb made of rock, not far from Golgotha. Joseph covered the opening of the tomb with a huge stone. This took place late Friday, the day Jesus died.

On the day we call Easter Sunday, two disciples were walking on the road from Jerusalem to a village named Emmaus. As they went along, a stranger came up and walked with them. The disciples told the stranger how sad they were about Jesus. "We had hoped," they said, "that he would be the one who was going to redeem Israel!" The stranger asked: "Was it not necessary for the Messiah to suffer these things and enter his glory?" He then explained all that the Bible said about Jesus. They finally came to the village. The two disciples begged the stranger to stay with them. He stayed. *"He sat at table with them, took the bread, and said the blessing; then he broke the bread and gave it to them. Their eyes were opened and they recognized him; but he disappeared from their sight."* It was JESUS!

The two disciples hurried straight back to Jerusalem. They had to tell the other disciples! But when they got there, the others already knew! "The Lord is RISEN!" the others said. "He has appeared to Simon!"

The two disciples then told about their visit from Jesus. It was *"like a fire burning in us when he ... explained the Scriptures to us,"* they said. They told how they had *"recognized the Lord when he broke the bread."* (Luke 24:13-35)

Read Matthew 28:9-10 – Jesus appears to the women.

Read Luke 24:36-43 – Jesus appears to the Eleven.

Read Matthew 28:16-20 – Jesus appears in Galilee.

Workshop

Words to Know

- NAZARETH: the village in Galilee where Jesus lived, with Mary and Joseph, while He was growing up.
- HOLY SPIRIT: God; the third Person of the Blessed Trinity.
- JOSEPH: the husband of Mary, the mother of Jesus. Saint Joseph was a carpenter (Matthew 13:55). So was Jesus (Mark 6:3).
- SAVIOR: the One who frees and saves His people; Jesus Christ.
- VIRGIN MARY: Mary is called *Virgin* because she became pregnant, but not in the ordinary way; with her consent, the Holy Spirit caused her to become Jesus' mother. Jesus is the only child Mary had.
- ABBA: "dearest Dad"; the name Jesus calls His Father.
- DISCIPLES: people Jesus calls to live with Him and be His followers.
- APOSTLES: the twelve people Jesus chose from among His disciples to take His place in a special way.
- HOLY THURSDAY: the day before Jesus died on the Cross; the day of the Last Supper.
- LAST SUPPER: Jesus' final meal with His Apostles; His Passover meal.
- PASSOVER MEAL: the sacred meal celebrating the night God spared His people before their Exodus from Egypt. (See pages 15 and 19.) At this meal, each family eats a roasted lamb. For Christians, Jesus is the Lamb who is sacrificed to God and eaten at each Holy Eucharist — read John 1:29-36; see also Isaiah 53:7, Acts 8:32, and 1 Peter 1:8-9.
- NEW COVENANT: the close, personal Covenant of love that Jesus' followers have with God.
- EUCHARIST: the sacred meal at which Jesus is present in His Passover (His Passion, Death, and Resurrection) as His followers share the meal in memory of Him.
- GETHSEMANE: a garden near the Mount of Olives outside the old east wall of Jerusalem; the place where Jesus prayed after the Last Supper.
- PONTIUS PILATE: the Roman governor who ruled the part of Israel called Judea from A.D. 26 to 36. During Jesus' lifetime, Israel was an occupied nation ruled by the Roman Empire.
- GOLGOTHA: a small hill outside the old northwest wall of Jerusalem where condemned criminals were executed by crucifixion. The word CALVARY comes from *Calvariae locus*, a Latin translation of *Golgotha*. Both words mean "Place of the Skull."
- GOOD FRIDAY: the day Jesus was crucified, died, and was buried.
- EASTER: the Sunday Jesus rose from the dead; the day celebrating Jesus' Passover from death to new Life.
- EMMAUS: a town which was about seven miles west of Jerusalem.
- REDEEM: In the Bible, God *redeems* His people by *freeing* them from slavery and enemies. Jesus redeems or frees us from evil so that we can love God and one another.
- SIMON: In Luke, chapter 24, Simon means Simon Peter, or Saint Peter.

Mini-test

1. Why did Joseph go to Bethlehem to register for the census? (Page 21) What does this tell you about Joseph's family tree?
2. How did Joseph learn that Mary's baby was very special? (Page 21)
3. How can you tell that Jesus was very special even as a child? How can you tell that obedience to parents is important to Jesus? (Page 22)
4. What do you know about God from Jesus' name for Him? What do you know about God from Jesus' stories in Saint Luke's Gospel? (Page 23)
5. Write, or say by heart, Jesus' two Great Commandments. (Page 24)
6. Read Jesus' two Great Commandments on page 24. Next, read the Ten Commandments on page 16. Which of the Ten Commandments are ways of loving God and neighbor?
7. When you help others, you are really helping Jesus. Write, or say by heart, Jesus' words about this truth. (Page 24)
8. What kind of people does Jesus love in a special way? Name three examples. (Page 25)
9. What gave Jesus' disciples the idea that it is very important to pray? (Page 26)
10. Write, or say by heart, the Our Father. (Page 26)
11. What does the Our Father say about forgiving? (Page 26) What does page 25 in this book say about forgiving?
12. What does the Our Father say about God's name? (Page 26) How can you honor the name of God? (See pages 16 and 12.)
13. How can you tell that, at the Last Supper, Jesus already knew He was going to die soon? (Page 27)
14. Why did Jesus wash the Apostles' feet at the Last Supper? (Page 27) Why did the Apostles need this example? (Read the Gospel of Saint Luke, 22:24-27.)
15. At Passover each year, Jewish people remember the Exodus — the time God saved the Hebrews and made them His Covenant people. What is there about the Eucharist that makes it Jesus' Passover meal? (Page 27)
16. How did God "seal" or start the new Covenant? (Pages 27 and 28)
17. What is the new Covenant? (Page 30)
18. Why did the Council vote to have Jesus put to death? (Page 28)
19. What does *Messiah* mean? (Page 19)
20. What did Jesus say when He admitted to Pilate that He is a king? What did Jesus mean by that? (Page 28)
21. Why did Pontius Pilate allow Jesus to be crucified? (Page 28)
22. Who buried the body of Jesus? (Page 29)
23. On what day of the week did Jesus die? On what day of the week did the "Stranger" appear? (Page 29)
24. The "Stranger" explained the Bible to the disciples. Then He broke bread and gave it to them. What does that remind you of? (Pages 29 and 27)
25. How is Jesus, the Risen Lord, with you today? (Page 29)

Write and Share at Home

1. Describe how Mary felt when she learned she was going to be the mother of Jesus.
2. Describe how Mary felt when she and Joseph discovered that twelve-year-old Jesus was lost. Describe how Joseph felt. (Boys, tell how Mary felt. Girls, tell how Joseph felt.)
3. Describe how Jesus felt about His *Abba*.
4. Write down three ways that you love yourself.
5. Write down the names of three "forgotten" people you know. What are you going to do to help these people? When are you going to do it?
6. Describe how Jesus, at the Last Supper, felt about His friends.
7. Describe how the Emmaus disciples felt when they were with the "Stranger."

Pray and Do

1. The Our Father takes two different forms in the Gospels (Matthew 6:9-13; Luke 11:2-4). Which form — Matthew's or Luke's — comes closest to the form Catholics use today? Compare them.
2. Here is the beautiful prayer, the Hail Mary. Find as many phrases of this prayer as you can in the first chapter of Saint Luke's Gospel. (Be sure everyone knows this prayer by heart.)

    Hail Mary, full of grace. The Lord is with thee. Blessed art thou among women, and blessed is the fruit of thy womb, Jesus. Holy Mary, Mother of God, pray for us sinners, now and at the hour of our death. Amen.

3. The 80-page booklet *Learning About Jesus* contains simple playlets about Jesus' life that children can act out. The booklet also contains stories and activities for home and school. Obtain *Learning About Jesus* for $1.95 plus 50¢ from Liguori Publications, One Liguori Drive, Liguori, Missouri 63057.

UNIT FOUR: YOU LIVE IN THE SPIRIT OF JESUS

19 When did the Father send the Holy Spirit? (Pentecost)

At the Last Supper, Jesus said good-bye to His Apostles. He was going home to the Father. He told the Apostles: "I will ask the Father, and he will give you another helper. . . . The Holy Spirit, whom the Father will send in my name, will teach you everything." (John 14:16, 26)

Forty days after He rose from the dead, Jesus told His disciples, " 'You will be filled with power when the Holy Spirit comes on you.' After saying this, he was taken up to heaven as they watched him." (Acts 1:8-9) This is called Jesus' Ascension into heaven.

Ten days later, the Apostles were all together in a room. "Suddenly there was a noise from the sky which sounded like a strong wind blowing, and it filled the whole house where they were sitting. Then they saw what looked like tongues of fire spreading out; and each person there was touched by a tongue. THEY WERE ALL FILLED WITH THE HOLY SPIRIT!" (Acts 2:2-4) This happened on Pentecost Sunday.

After the Spirit filled them, the Apostles went outside. They began to tell people about Jesus. That day, there were many people in Jerusalem who had come from other countries. These people spoke foreign languages. When the Apostles talked, the crowd was stunned. Each person heard the Apostles talking in his own language! The Spirit was here at last, helping the Apostles. Now they could tell the whole world about Jesus!

Read Acts 2:32-33 – Peter speaks of the Spirit's coming.

Read Acts 8:14-17 – Samaritans receive the Spirit.

Read Acts 11:15-17 – Peter tells how the Spirit comes to non-Jews.

20 How does the Spirit live in you? (Grace; Faith; Hope; Love)

On the day of Pentecost, the Apostles were filled with the Holy Spirit. All of Jesus' followers are given the Spirit. "God has poured out his love into our hearts by means of the Holy Spirit, who is God's gift to us." (Romans 5:5)

In its Decree on the Apostolate of the Laity, the Second Vatican Council says the following about faith, hope, and charity:

Faith: "Only by the light of faith and by meditation on the word of God can one always and everywhere recognize God in whom 'we live, and move, and have our being' (Acts 17:28), seek His will in every event, see Christ in all men. . . ." (Laity, 4)

Hope: "They who have this faith . . . find strength in hope, convinced that 'the sufferings of the present time are not worthy to be compared with the glory to come that will be revealed in us' (Rom 1:18)." (Laity, 4)

Love: "Impelled by divine charity, they do good to all men, especially to those of the household of the faith (cf. Gal 6:10), laying aside 'all malice and all deceit and pretense, and envy, and all slander' (1 Pet 2:1), and thereby they draw men to Christ." (Laity, 4)

The Spirit lives in your heart and soul. The Spirit makes you alive with God's special Life called GRACE. God's Life of grace makes you one of God's family. It makes Jesus your own Brother. It makes heaven your home.

With the Spirit in you, you live a life of *faith*. You say "Yes" to what Jesus teaches. Jesus teaches that God, your Father, loves you very much. He teaches that when you love your neighbor, you love Jesus Himself. You say "Yes, Lord, I believe!" You have FAITH.

With the Spirit in you, you live a life of *hope*. God kept His early promises by giving Israel the Covenant. God has kept His greatest promise by sending Jesus, who died and then rose again. God has promised that you will live with Him forever. You *trust* God to keep that promise too. You have HOPE.

With the Spirit in you, you live a life of *love*. You love the Lord your God with all your heart. You love your fellowman as yourself. You love Jesus by loving others, especially those who need help the most. You have LOVE.

34

21 What seven helps does the Spirit give you? (Gifts of the Spirit)

The Holy Spirit is God's great Gift to you. The Spirit gives you seven special helps called "Gifts of the Spirit." These Gifts are:

WISDOM. Do you remember the last time you prayed or did something for God because you really wanted to? When you did that, the Spirit helped you to be *wise*.

UNDERSTANDING. Do you remember the last time something from the Bible or from religion class really impressed you? When that happened, the Spirit helped you to *understand*.

COUNSEL. Do you remember the last time you decided to be a better Christian? When you did that, the Spirit *counseled* you in your heart.

FORTITUDE. Do you remember the last time you had the courage to do something difficult? When you did that, the Spirit helped you to be *strong*.

KNOWLEDGE. What is the most important truth you know about your life — or about God or your parents or others? You see that truth so well because the Spirit helps you to *know*.

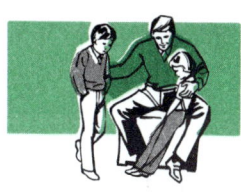

LOVING AFFECTION (PIETY). Who are the people in your life you love the most? You love these persons so much because the Spirit helps you to be *affectionate*.

ADORATION and PRAISE (FEAR OF THE LORD). Do you remember the last time you told God how great He is — or told Him how happy you are to be alive? When you did that, the Spirit helped you to *praise*.

Read Acts 10:44-48 – God pours out His gift, the Spirit, upon the people.

Read Isaiah 11:2-3 – the Spirit's gifts.

Read 1 Corinthians 12:6-11 – gifts the Spirit gives to some for the good of others.

22 Why are you one of God's family? (Trinity)

The Holy Spirit lives in your heart and soul. With the Spirit in you, you "share the divine nature." (2 Peter 1:4) You are a member of *God's own family.*

God is your FATHER. You are His son, His daughter. You are a sister, a brother, to Jesus. In the Spirit, you are "family" with the Father and His Son, Jesus.

Read Matthew 5:43-48 – God is Father, we are brothers and sisters.

Read Hebrews 1:1-3 – the Son is the Word, God's image, through whom God creates the universe.

Read Romans 5:5 – the love in our hearts is from God's gift, the Holy Spirit.

God is the Speaker. You are God's listener. The WORD that God speaks to you is JESUS. When you listen to Jesus, you listen to God Himself, the Father of Jesus.

God is your Life-giving SPIRIT. All the loving things you do are spiritual. God's Life grows in you like a flower. One day this flower will blossom open and you will see Jesus and the Father.

The FATHER, SON, and HOLY SPIRIT are even closer than a family. They are so closely related that they are really ONE GOD. The one God is *with* you and *in* you as three divine Persons, THE BLESSED TRINITY.

Workshop

Words to Know

- ASCENSION: Jesus' being lifted up into heaven where He now "sits at the right hand of God the Father." Ascension Thursday is the 40th day after Easter.
- PENTECOST: the Sunday — 50 days after Easter — when the Apostles were "filled with the Holy Spirit." Pentecost has been called "the birthday of the Church."
- GRACE: God's gift, the Holy Spirit; the Life of the Spirit by which you "share the divine nature." Two aspects of this Life are habitual grace (the state of sanctifying grace) and actual grace (divine helps given for the performing of acts).
- FAITH, HOPE, LOVE: the three divine virtues that you have along with the Life of grace.
- GIFTS OF THE SPIRIT: the gifts listed on page 35. Loving Affection is also called Piety. Fear of the Lord is another term for Adoration and Praise. Other gifts of the Spirit, called *charisms,* are listed in 1 Corinthians 12:6-11.
- WORD OF GOD: Jesus, the Word made flesh (John 1:14). In the New Testament, "the word" usually means the gospel — the Good News. According to Vatican Council II, "Sacred Scripture is the Word of God inasmuch as it is consigned to writing under the inspiration of the divine Spirit." (*Revelation*, 9)
- BLESSED TRINITY: the three divine Persons — Father, Son, and Spirit — who share the one divine nature.

Mini-test

1. When did the Holy Spirit come to the Apostles? (Page 33)
2. What happened to the Apostles when the Spirit came? What happened to the crowd? (Page 33)
3. What is grace? What does grace do? (Page 34)
4. How can you tell that you have faith? (Page 34)
5. How can you tell that you have hope? (Page 34)
6. How can you tell that you have love? (Page 34)
7. Name the seven Gifts of the Spirit. (Page 35)
8. Explain what the Spirit does in each Gift. (Page 35)
9. What makes you a member of God's family? (Page 36)
10. If God is your Father, what does that make you? (Page 36)
11. If God is the Speaker, what does that make you? What Word does God speak? (Page 36)
12. If God is your Life-giving Spirit, what does that say about you? (Page 36)
13. What is the Blessed Trinity? (Page 36)

Write and Share at Home

1. Describe how the Apostles felt when they became "filled with the Holy Spirit."
2. In your own words, tell how you feel about God. Give *your* feelings, *your* attitudes, *your* ideas.
3. Share your answers to the questions on page 35.
4. The Good News is that you really do belong to God's family. Jesus is your own Brother. How do you feel about that?

Pray and Do

Here is an old and beautiful prayer of praise to the Blessed Trinity. Be sure that you know this prayer by heart. Pick a time when you will say it every day.

Glory be to the Father, and to the Son, and to the Holy Spirit, as it was in the beginning, is now, and ever shall be, world without end. Amen.

UNIT FIVE: YOU LIVE IN THE CHURCH OF JESUS

23 Who makes the Church the Body of Jesus? (Risen Jesus)

In the Bible, Acts of the Apostles tells about a man named Saul. Saul did not like Christians. He thought that the Christians worshiped a Jesus who was dead. Saul did not know that Jesus is risen and alive.

Saul was traveling from Jerusalem to Damascus. He was on a mission to capture some Christians. As Saul neared Damascus, there was a flash of light. Saul found himself flat on the ground. He heard a voice: *"Saul, Saul, why do you persecute ME?"*
Saul said: "Who are you, Lord?"
"I am JESUS, whom you persecute," the voice said.

From that moment on, Saul could not see. He was blind. Some Christians took him to their home in Damascus. For three days he did not eat or drink anything. Then a man named Ananias came and laid his hands on Saul's head. Suddenly, Saul was *filled with the Holy Spirit!* Suddenly, he could see again! Saul was then baptized as a Christian. From then on, he was known as Paul. (Acts 9:1-19)

For the rest of his life Saint Paul worked as an Apostle for Jesus. He always remembered that voice saying, *"I am JESUS whom you persecute."* That message was God's truth. When Saul had captured Christians and thrown them into prison, he had been throwing JESUS into prison! *Jesus is RISEN. He LIVES in His followers. The followers of Jesus are HIS BODY, the Church.*

Read Acts 9:1-19, 22:5-16, 26:12-18 – the conversion of Saint Paul.

Saint Augustine wrote: "Let us rejoice and give thanks that we have become not only Christians but Christ... we have become Christ. For if He is the Head, we are the members; He and we are the complete man..." (in Pope Paul VI, Ecclesiam Suam, 37).

Read 1 Corinthians 12:12-30 – we are one body.

24 Who makes your family "the Church"?
(Jesus; Family)

Jesus' followers are His Body, the Church. Jesus lives in His followers all over the world. For you, Jesus lives especially in one place: He lives in *your family*. Your family is the Body of Jesus at home.

Priests and Sisters and Brothers are Church people. They work for Jesus. Parents and children are Church people too. Parents do not have the same jobs as priests and Sisters and Brothers. But the work parents do is work for Jesus. Jesus lives in His followers' families. He lives in *your* family.

Some people do not think of their family as Jesus' Body. They say: "Our family has problems. We fight. My brother keeps getting in trouble. My father is out of work. We have no money." Jesus says: "You are My Body. I love you and I live in you."

Jesus is always with you. You can feel His love in your family when you . . .

— Try to *believe* that God your Father loves everyone in your family with His whole heart.

— Try to *see* Jesus in each other. When you help each other, you are helping Jesus. Whatever happens to any member of your family, happens to JESUS.

Pope Paul VI wrote: ". . . the family has well deserved the beautiful name of 'domestic Church.' This means that there should be found in every Christian family the various aspects of the entire Church" (On Evangelization, 71).

The Second Vatican Council said that parents are "the first and foremost educators of their children. Their role as educators is so decisive that scarcely anything can compensate for their failure in it" (Christian Education, 3).

25 Who makes your parish a family? (Jesus in the Eucharist)

The family that lives together eats together. Family meals are important. Sharing food helps family members to be closer to each other.

Your parish is a family because all of you share a special meal. That meal is the Holy Eucharist. Every Sunday your parish family comes together in church. You share food together. The food is Jesus Himself, the Bread of Life. When Jesus comes to you, you become closer to all the others who share this Bread. You are all one Body. *"Because there is one bread, all of us, though many, are one body, because we all share the same loaf." (1 Corinthians 10:17)*

The people in your parish are like your aunts and uncles and cousins. Jesus lives in them and Jesus lives in you. You are like relatives. When you share the Bread of Life together, you become *closer* relatives.

Your parish family does many things together. You pray and sing together. You play sports and games together. You have school and learn together. You help the poor and the missions. You do all these things because you love Jesus.

You share the Eucharist and you help others. Your parish becomes a closer family. Jesus' Body grows and becomes stronger.

MAKE THE PARISH a COMMUNITY OF FAMILIES

The Second Vatican Council says that "the Eucharistic Action is the very heartbeat of the congregation of the faithful over which the priest presides" (Ministry and Life of Priests, 5).

The Second Vatican Council says: "No Christian community . . . can be built up unless it has its basis and center in the celebration of the most Holy Eucharist" (Ministry and Life of Priests, 6).

26 What do One, Holy, Catholic, Apostolic mean? (Marks of Church)

Every Sunday, in the Creed at Mass, you say: *We believe in one, holy, catholic, and apostolic Church.* Do you know what these words mean?

ONE. The Pope and the Catholic Bishops keep God's people *together*. Because of them, we are *one* family. There is "one Lord, one faith, one baptism, one God and Father of all." (Ephesians 4:5) All the people who believe this truth are *together*. We are *one*. The Holy Eucharist is the "one bread." All who share this bread are one.

HOLY. All of us are sinners. Still, we are God's holy people because we belong to Jesus — because the Holy Spirit lives in our hearts — because the Father forgives us our sins, as we forgive those who sin against us.

CATHOLIC. *Catholic* means "for everybody everywhere." The Church is called "Catholic" because the Good News of Jesus is for everybody everywhere. The Church is called "Catholic" also because it *is* all over the world.

APOSTOLIC. The Pope and the Catholic Bishops take the place of Saint Peter and the Apostles. The Church is "apostolic" because it has had Popes and Bishops as its leaders ever since the time of Jesus. The Church is APOSTOLIC because we follow Jesus. We are trying to become more closely ONE, more HOLY, and more CATHOLIC.

Speaking of "the unique Church of Christ which in the Creed we avow as one, holy, catholic, and apostolic," the Second Vatican Council says: "This Church, constituted and organized in the world as a society, subsists in the Catholic Church . . . although many elements of sanctification and of truth can be found outside of her visible structure" (The Church, 8).

About unity in the Church, the Second Vatican Council says: "The bonds which unite the faithful are mightier than anything which divides them. Hence, let there be unity in what is necessary, freedom in what is unsettled, and charity in any case" (Church in the Modern World, 92).

Workshop

Words to Know

- DAMASCUS: a city in Syria, northeast of Jerusalem.
- CHURCH AT HOME: "The family is, so to speak, the domestic Church." (Vatican Council II, *The Church,* 11)
- POPE: the *visible* head of Jesus' Body, the Church. Jesus chose Saint Peter as head of the Twelve Apostles. Peter was the first Pope. Since the time of Jesus, there have been 264 Popes. Through the Pope, as head of the Bishops, the Holy Spirit keeps the Church faithful to the teaching of Jesus. The Pope speaks the truth infallibly — without possibility of error — when he speaks *ex cathedra* on matters of faith and morals. The Pope's mission from Jesus is to lead and strengthen the Church in its calling to be one, holy, catholic, and apostolic. The true Head of the Church is Jesus Christ.
- BISHOPS: As Bishop of Rome, the Pope has authority over all other Bishops in the world. As the official leaders of the Church, the Bishops take the place of the Twelve Apostles. Bishops possess the fullness of Holy Orders; only they can give Holy Orders to others. Ordinarily, a Bishop conducts the temporal and spiritual affairs of a diocese. (An *archbishop* is the Bishop of the main diocese in a group of dioceses called a province.) Priests and deacons in a diocese work under the authority of their leader, the local Bishop.

Mini-test

1. How did Saul learn that Jesus lives in His followers? (Page 39)
2. Why is your family "the Body of Jesus at home"? (Page 40)
3. How does Jesus make your parish a family? (Page 41)
4. What do you mean when you say "We believe in one, holy, catholic, and apostolic Church"? (Page 42)

Write and Share at Home

1. God your Father loves everyone in your family with His whole heart. How do you feel about that?
2. Jesus lives in your family. Whatever happens to any one of you, happens to Him. How do you feel about that?

Pray and Do

1. Memorize Saint Paul's words in 1 Corinthians 10:17.
2. Find out all you can about the Pope and your local Bishop. A good source is the CATHOLIC ALMANAC, published yearly in a paperback edition by Our Sunday Visitor, Inc.

UNIT SIX: YOU MEET JESUS IN BIBLE, PRAYER

27 What is the Bible?
(Old and New Testaments; Inspired Word)

Before you read this page, get out your Bible.

The Bible you are looking at is a set of books. The Bible has two main parts: the *Old* Testament and the *New* Testament.

The *Old* Testament books tell about God and Israel. They tell how God helped Israel grow up to become His Covenant people. There are 46 books in the Old Testament writings. These books are in four sections. Look on the contents page in the front of your Bible. The first section (the Five Books of the Law) starts with *Genesis*. The second section (the Historical Books) starts with *Joshua*. The third section (the Wisdom Books) starts with *Job*. The fourth section in the Old Testament (the Prophets) starts with the Book of *Isaiah*.

The New Testament is all about Jesus. The four Gospels tell about His life and death. They tell about His rising from the dead and being alive now in His Body, the Church. Look on your contents page. First come the four Gospels of Matthew, Mark, Luke, and John. Then comes Acts of the Apostles, which is really "Book Two" of Luke's Gospel. Next come the Letters (or Epistles) of Saint Paul and the Letters of James, Peter, John, and Jude. The last book is Revelation. There are 27 books in the New Testament.

There are 73 books in the Catholic Bible. These books were written by people with special help from the Holy Spirit. That help is called *divine inspiration*. The Bible is the *inspired* word of God.

Hold each section of the Bible together and mark the edges with a felt-tip pen. Use a different color on each section. (Or, instead of pens, use bookmarks.)

Memorize the titles of the five books of the Law.

28 How do you pray with the Bible?
(Reading, praying the Bible)

You can read the Bible alone by yourself. That is a good thing to do. You can read the Bible and talk to Jesus about it. This is called praying with the Bible.

You can use the Bible to pray in a group. It can be a big group like your whole class. It can be a small group like you and your family at home. When you pray with the Bible in a group, Jesus is there with you. He says: *"Where two or three come together in my name, I am there with them."* (Matthew 18:20)

Here is a way you can read and pray with the Bible.

1. Be silent for a moment. Think of Jesus. He is right here with you. Say the Our Father aloud together with Jesus.

2. Together, choose one person to read aloud. Let the reader choose a favorite story from the Bible. Or choose the story together. Listen to the story very carefully.

3. After the reading, be silent for a moment. Ask: *Lord, what are You telling me in this story?* Talk about it with Jesus or the Father or the Holy Spirit.

4. Take turns sharing your answers to the question you asked yourselves. Listen very carefully to what each person says.

5. To finish, take turns saying a very short prayer. Say something like this: "Thank You, Jesus, for telling me this story." Or: "Father, help us to do what You told us in the story."

Have each person answer in writing: My favorite story in the Bible is. . . .

After praying together with the Bible, have each person answer: The thing I liked best about praying together this time was. . . .

29 What are the mysteries of the Rosary? (Summary of the Gospel)

The rosary is a "compendium (a short explanation) of the entire Gospel." Our Holy Father, the Pope, said that. What he means is this: When you pray the rosary, you pray the whole story of Jesus' life, death, and rising. Each part of the story is called a *mystery*. Here are the *mysteries of the rosary*:

The Joyful Mysteries
1. The angel tells Mary she will be the Mother of Jesus.
2. Mary visits and helps her cousin Elizabeth.
3. Jesus is born in a stable in Bethlehem.
4. Jesus is presented in the Temple.
5. Jesus is found in the Temple.

The Sorrowful Mysteries
1. Jesus suffers agony in the garden of Gethsemane.
2. Jesus is scourged at the pillar.
3. Jesus is crowned with thorns.
4. Jesus carries the Cross to Calvary.
5. Jesus dies on the Cross to save the world.

The Glorious Mysteries
1. Jesus rises from the dead.
2. Jesus ascends into heaven.
3. The Apostles are filled with the Spirit at Pentecost.
4. Jesus' Mother Mary is taken up into heaven.
5. Mary is crowned queen of heaven and earth.

In three groups of five, have each person recite one mystery in the proper sequence.

Have each person memorize and recite the fifteen mysteries.

30 How do you pray the Rosary?
(The five-decade Rosary)

Before you begin this page, get out your rosary. Follow the numbers shown with the rosary on this page.

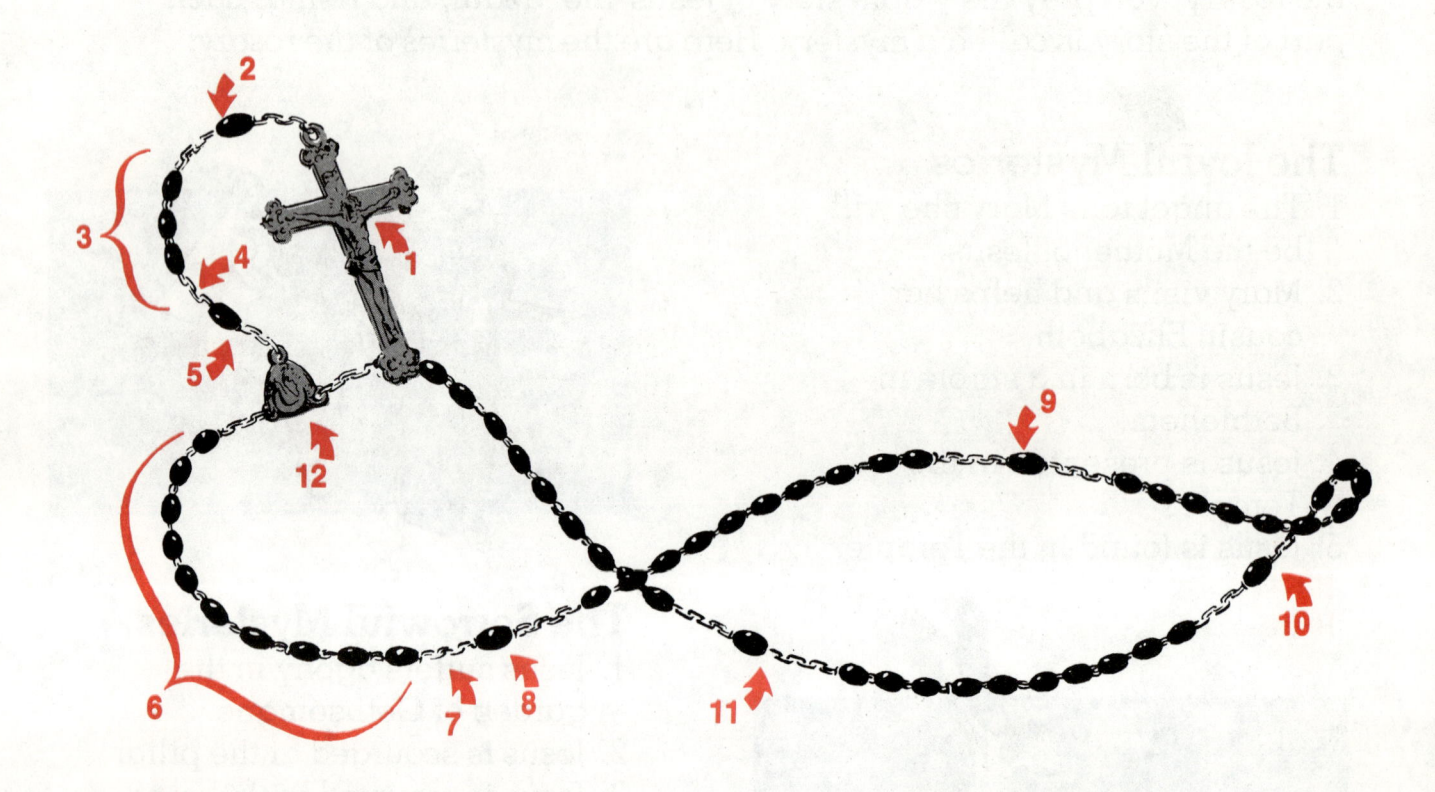

1. Begin by making the Sign of the Cross with the crucifix. Then pray the Apostles' Creed.
2. Pray one Our Father.
3. Pray three Hail Marys.
4. Pray one Glory Be to the Father.
5. Say or think of the *first mystery* (Joyful, Sorrowful, or Glorious). Then pray one Our Father.
6. Pray ten Hail Marys, thinking of the first mystery.
7. Pray one Glory Be to the Father.
8. Say or think of the *second mystery*. Pray one Our Father, ten Hail Marys, and one Glory Be to the Father. (Do the same thing for numbers 9, 10, and 11 — the third, fourth, and fifth mysteries.)
12. At the end of the rosary, many Catholics like to pray the Hail, Holy Queen.

Together, with rosaries in hand, go through the steps of praying the five-decade rosary.

Together, using page 52 if needed, pray the Hail, Holy Queen.

31 How do you pray mini-prayers? (Prayers from the Bible)

Every day you hear sayings like "Oh, wow!" — "What's happening?" — "Let's go!" Mini-prayers are like that. They are short and quick. With mini-prayers, you can pray 100 times a day.

The Bible is filled with mini-prayers. The thing to do is to choose your own favorite ones. To give you a head start, here are a few mini-prayers from the Bible.

- I believe! (Mark 9:24)
- Blessed be God! (Psalm 68:35)
- Lord, my savior! (Psalm 38:22)
- I will thank You forever! (Psalm 52:9)
- Thanks be to God! (Romans 6:17)
- Help me, O Lord my God! (Psalm 109:26)
- Come and rescue me, God! (Psalm 70:1)
- Lord, have mercy on us! (Matthew 20:31)
- Jesus, Son of David, have mercy on me! (Mark 10:47)
- Come, Lord Jesus! (Revelation 22:20)

Have each person choose – or make up – a favorite mini-prayer.

A mini-prayer can be just one word. Here are some good ones: *God, Father, Lord, Jesus, Mary.*

It takes only a second to say a mini-prayer. You can pray this way anytime — when you get up in the morning — when you open a door — when you sit down — when you change clothes. Choose your favorite times and places. Pray mini-prayers every day.

32 How can you learn to live the Good News? (Evangelization)

You can know the Good News by reading the Bible. But *knowing* the Good News is just the beginning. The News is really Good only when you *live* it and *share* it.

Home is where you learn to share the Good News. When you help your mother or father, your home is the School of Good News. When you forgive your brother or sister, your family is the School of Good News.

Your family shares love. But you can become an even more loving family — an even better School of Good News. You can do this by having "family meetings."

Pick a date and time for your next (or first) family meeting.

After your family meeting, have each person answer: What I liked best about our family meeting was. . . .

Here is what family meetings are. The family meets on the same evening every week. The meeting lasts about an hour. The family reads and prays with the Bible. (Page 46 shows how you can read and pray with the Bible.) The family spends time talking about family matters. You make plans. You discuss problems. You share feelings. You respect and *listen* to each other very carefully. The family may want to play a game together. Or you may want to work together on a family hobby or project. You may want to have a special snack treat. The meeting ends with a short prayer.

You live the Good News by sharing love. Sharing love begins at home. Family meetings help you to share more love.

Workshop

Words to Know

- EVANGELIZATION: To *evangelize* means to know, to love, to live by, and to share the Gospel with others in word and deed. To *be* evangelized means to become a lover and sharer of the Gospel by experiencing the Christian faith and love-filled lives of others. Pope Paul VI pointed out that we begin "by being evangelized" ourselves, and that we hand on the Gospel "by transmitting to another person one's personal experience of faith." *(On Evangelization*, 15 and 46)
- DIVINE INSPIRATION: "All Scripture is inspired by God." (2 Timothy 3:16) The people who wrote the Bible wrote it in their own words, in their own way. But God influenced or inspired them to write *all* that He wanted them to say, and *only* what He wanted them to say. (See Vatican Council II, *Revelation*, 11.)

Mini-test

1. What are the four sections of the Old Testament? (Page 45)
2. What is the Old Testament about? (Page 45)
3. Who wrote the New Testament? (Page 45)
4. What is the New Testament about? (Page 45)
5. What is divine inspiration? (Pages 45 and 51)
6. How do you know Jesus is there with you when you pray in a group? (Page 46)
7. Recite the Joyful Mysteries; the Sorrowful Mysteries; the Glorious Mysteries. (Page 47)
8. How do you pray the rosary? (Page 48)
9. Why are family meetings a good thing to do? (Page 50)

Write and Share at Home

1. What is your favorite Bible story? What is your favorite mini-prayer from the Bible? Tell why you like them.
2. Tell what you liked about the first family meeting you had in your family.

Pray and Do

1. In your Bible, go through the Book of Psalms and pick out some good mini-prayers. Write them down on a piece of paper. Keep the paper with you. Use a different mini-prayer, every day.
2. Pray five decades of the rosary, with either the Joyful, Sorrowful, or Glorious Mysteries.
3. Memorize this beautiful prayer to Mary. Say it when you finish praying the rosary.

   Hail, holy queen, mother of mercy, our life, our sweetness, and our hope. To you we cry, poor banished children of Eve; to you we send up our sighs, mourning and weeping in this valley of tears. Turn then, O most gracious advocate, your eyes of mercy toward us, and after this our exile, show unto us the blessed fruit of your womb, Jesus. O clement, O loving, O sweet virgin Mary.
   Pray for us, O holy Mother of God.
   (Response) That we may be made worthy of the promises of Christ.

4. In each monthly issue, MARRIAGE AND FAMILY LIVING magazine publishes a section called "Family Night," which offers ideas for weekly family meetings. Write or call: Subscription Service, Marriage, St. Meinrad, IN 47577. Phone: (812) 357-8251.

UNIT SEVEN: YOU MEET JESUS IN LITURGY

33 What is a sacrament? (Sign; Meeting with Jesus; Grace)

As children, your parents learned this truth: *A sacrament is an outward sign instituted by Christ to give grace.* A sacrament is a special sign from Jesus that helps you to live His Life in the Church.

Jesus gave His Church *seven* sacraments. They are called: *Baptism; Confirmation; Holy Eucharist; Reconciliation* (or *Penance); Anointing of the Sick; Matrimony;* and *Holy Orders.*

Each sacrament has an *outward sign.* In the Holy Eucharist, you receive Jesus as the Bread of Life. *Bread* is the sign of Jesus in the Eucharist. Each sacrament has its own sign.

A sacrament is *a meeting with Jesus.* He comes to you each time you share in a sacrament. He *calls* you to welcome Him. You *answer* Jesus by having faith in Him. You say in your heart: "Lord, I believe You are here in this sacrament. Please bring us closer to You. Bring me closer to my dear Family, the Church. Help us to grow in love as Your Family."

The Second Vatican Council says: "By His power He is present in the sacraments, so that when a man baptizes it is really Christ Himself who baptizes" (Liturgy, 7).

Each sacrament gives its own wonderful grace. Through the sign of bread in the Eucharist, Jesus comes to you as Life-giving *food.* Through the words of forgiveness in Reconciliation, Jesus *heals* you from sin which makes you unhappy. In its own special way, each sacrament brings you Jesus' Life. All seven sacraments bring you closer to Jesus and to your Family, His Body.

Sacraments are signs that "contain the grace they signify" (Council of Trent). Each sacrament produces its grace through the humanity of Jesus. As the Gospel says, "power was going out from him and healing them all" (Luke 6:19).

34 How do sacraments help you?
(Helps on the journey of life)

Your life is a journey home to the Father. For your journey, there are *three* sacraments of initiation. *Initiation* means "getting started" on your journey.

• At BAPTISM you are *born* into Jesus' Body, the Church.
• At CONFIRMATION you become a *grown-up* member of Jesus' Body.
• At First EUCHARIST you start to share *fully* in the Mass, Jesus' Passover journey to new, risen Life. Baptism is your crossing through the Red Sea. Holy Communion is the manna you eat on your desert journey to heaven.

The ultimate goal of all the sacraments, linked with the central sacrament of Eucharist, is com-union with God in the Spirit-filled Body of Jesus.

Read John 6:49-55 – the Eucharist as food and drink on the journey.

On your journey home, there are *two* sacraments of *reconciliation* and *healing*.

• Sin makes a person weak and less loving toward Jesus and His Family. In RECONCILIATION, Jesus makes you strong and loving.

• ANOINTING helps people who are old, or sick, to have better health. If God wants them to go home to Him soon, Anointing strengthens them for this final journey.

Jesus may call you to serve the Father by being married or by being a priest or deacon. For these two ways of life, there are two sacraments of *commitment*.

• In MATRIMONY, a man and a woman promise to love each other all their lives, just as Jesus loves His people, the Church.

• In HOLY ORDERS Bishops, priests, and deacons promise to help God's people on their journey to the Father. They serve the people by *preaching God's Word* to them, by *sharing the sacraments* with them, and by *leading them* to be a closer FAMILY.

35 How does Baptism change you?
(New birth; Life in the Church)

Before you were born, you were alive inside your mother's body. But you did not have a name yet. Your family could not see you. They could not feed you or take care of you.

After you were born, your family could see you. They gave you your name. They took care of you and made you happy.

After you were born, your family took you to church. Now all the people in church could see their new family member, you. At church the priest *baptized* you. He poured water on your head. He said: *"I baptize you in the name of the Father, and of the Son, and of the Holy Spirit."* The pouring of the water was the sign that you now belong to the Father, Son, and Holy Spirit. The priest then said: *"God the Father of our Lord Jesus Christ has freed you from sin, given you a new birth by water and the Holy Spirit, and welcomed you into his holy people."*

BAPTISM *freed you from sin.* Because of Baptism you belong to Jesus. You are freed from original sin. By living as a member of Jesus, you help others to be free from sin.

BAPTISM *gave you a new birth and welcomed you into God's holy people, the Church.* At Baptism you were born into your family, the Church of Jesus. You became a Catholic member of the Christian family. All Christians are like relatives. But Catholics are like members of your very own family.

All baptized persons (including baptized Christians who are not Catholics) share "a sacramental bond linking all who have been reborn by means of it" (Vatican Council II, Decree on Ecumenism, 22). We are brothers and sisters.

Men and women in religious communities live a life "deeply rooted in their baptismal consecration" (Vatican Council II, Decree on Religious Life, 5).

36 How does Confirmation change you?
(Spirit; Growth)

Baptism is the sacrament that helped you to be *born* into the Church. Confirmation is the sacrament that helps you to *grow up* in the Church.

Jesus told His disciples: "You will be filled with power when the Holy Spirit comes on you." (Acts 1:8) On Pentecost Sunday, "They were all filled with the Holy Spirit." (Acts 2:4) That is what happens when you are confirmed. The Bishop, or your pastor, says to you: *"Be sealed with the Gift of the Holy Spirit."* You are filled with the Spirit.

Read Acts 8:14-17 – Samaritans receive the Spirit when Peter and John lay hands on them.

Review the Gifts of the Spirit on page 35.

Baptism and Confirmation are connected. The grace of Baptism = that of being a child of God in His family. The grace of Confirmation = that of strength to give adult witness within the family and beyond it.

When you are confirmed, your family and fellow Catholics are there with you. By being there, they say: "WE CONFIRM YOU. You are now an adult member of the family. Now you can confirm *us*. By sharing the Good News, you can help us to grow as Jesus' Body."

In Confirmation, *the Spirit* says "YES" to Jesus' Life in you. *Your fellow Catholics* say: "YES, you are now an adult member of the family." *You* say: "YES, the Spirit really does live in me. YES, I want to confirm my fellow Catholics by the example I give. YES, I want to confirm my family as Jesus' Body by helping and forgiving. YES to the Spirit."

You are born only once in Baptism. You become an adult only once in Confirmation. But you never have to stop growing. You can grow and grow in the Gifts of the Spirit. You can always keep confirming your fellow Catholics.

37 How does the Eucharist change you?
(Bread; Body; Life)

At the Last Supper, Jesus broke some bread and gave a piece to each Apostle. He said: *"This is my body which is given for you. Do this in memory of me."* (Luke 22:19)

The next day, Jesus died on the Cross. The following Sunday, two disciples were walking to Emmaus. A stranger came up and walked with them. When they reached the village, they sat down to eat. The Stranger "broke the bread and gave it to them." When he did that, they realized who He was. Then He disappeared from sight. Later, the other disciples said: *"The Lord is RISEN!"* (Luke 24:13-35)

Here are some things to remember about the Holy Eucharist.

• When you receive Holy Communion, you are receiving the body and blood of Jesus. Through the sign of bread, Jesus is really and truly *with you* and *in you*.

• Before He died, Jesus' body was like your body. He could be sick and get hurt. Now Jesus is risen. His body cannot be hurt. He can be in many places at one time. Jesus is in every sacred Host.

• Saint Paul said: *"Because there is the one bread, all of us, though many, are one body."* (1 Corinthians 10:17) In Holy Communion, you share Jesus' body with others. This sharing brings you closer to Jesus. It helps all of us to be a stronger, more loving Body of Jesus.

Read 1 Corinthians 10:16-17 and 11:23-26 – the earliest written statements of what the Eucharistic meal is and does for us.

Read John 6:53-58 – a Gospel statement of what sharing the Eucharistic bread does for us.

For a rich and poetic expression of the meaning of the Holy Eucharist, read the text of the Mass for the feast of Corpus Christi (Thursday after Trinity Sunday).

38 How does Reconciliation change you? (Penance; Absolution)

Zacchaeus was a crook. He became rich by cheating people. No one liked Zacchaeus. His sins against people had made him a lonely, unhappy man.

Jesus knew that Zacchaeus wanted to make up for his sins. So Jesus *forgave* Zacchaeus. He went and had a meal at Zacchaeus' house. Zacchaeus was overjoyed. He told Jesus: "If I have cheated anyone, I will pay him back four times as much." When He heard that, Jesus said: "Salvation has come to this house today." (Luke 19:1-10)

Sometimes we do things that keep us from being friends with others. That is when we need Jesus to forgive us in *the sacrament of Reconciliation*. Jesus helps us to make up for our sins. He brings us God's mercy. He brings salvation.

Contrition = sorrow and aversion for past sins with the resolve not to sin again. Perfect contrition = present when the motive is love of God, the highest Good, for His own sake. Imperfect contrition = present when the motive is not love of God but some other motive referring to God, such as the hatefulness of sin. In the sacrament of Reconciliation, imperfect contrition is sufficient for the remission of serious sin.

Doing the penance which the priest gives in Reconciliation is called satisfaction.

When the priest gives absolution, he ends by saying "I absolve you from your sins in the name of the Father, and of the Son, and of the Holy Spirit."

In Reconciliation you meet with Jesus. You talk to the priest. With Jesus and the priest you do four things:

• You CONFESS your sins. You think of God's merciful love. You think of your sins that need forgiveness. You tell those sins to the priest.

• You have CONTRITION. You are really sorry for your sins. You do not want to sin ever again.

• You do PENANCE. Like Zacchaeus, you make up for any harm you may have done to others. The priest gives you a penance to do. Doing this penance helps you to love.

• You receive ABSOLUTION. The priest tells you that you are forgiven. This is called absolution. Absolution is the sign that Jesus Himself has forgiven your sins.

39 How do you celebrate Reconciliation? (The rite of Penance)

You can celebrate Reconciliation in *a group* with a priest. Or, you can celebrate Reconciliation *alone* with the priest.

In a group (communal) celebration, you follow these steps:

1. The group sings an opening hymn and greets Father.
2. Father prays an opening prayer.
3. The group listens to a Bible reading and a homily.
4. You examine your conscience quietly.
5. The group makes a general confession (for example, *I confess to almighty God*).
6. The group shows sorrow for sin by praying a litany or singing a song. The group then prays the Our Father.
7. When it is your turn, you go to confession to Father.
8. At the end, Father prays a prayer of thanksgiving and gives the group a final blessing.

Even at a group celebration, you go to confession *alone* to Father. You do this in a *confessional* or in a *reconciliation room*. Here is how it goes:

1. Father welcomes you. You make the Sign of the Cross.
2. Father asks you to trust in God.
3. Father may read some words from the Bible.
4. You confess your sins. You tell Father about them.
5. You make an act of contrition.
6. Father tells you how to be a better Catholic.
7. Father gives you a penance.
8. Father gives you absolution. He extends his hands over you.
9. Together you and Father thank God for His mercy. Then Father gives you a final blessing.

For the detailed procedure of the sacrament, consult the official text in The Rites of the Catholic Church.

40 Who should be anointed?
(Sickness; Healing; Getting ready)

Sometimes people become very sick. They think: "Maybe I am going to die." When a person is that sick, it is time for the sacrament of Anointing.

At the sacrament of Anointing, a sick person meets Jesus. This is a very special meeting. The sick person may think: "Lord, I am really sick. If it is time for me to come to you in heaven, please help me to be ready. If you want me to stay on earth, please help me to get well."

Anointing can help a person to get well. In the Bible, the Letter of Saint James says: "Is there anyone who is sick? He should call the church elders, who will pray for him and rub oil on him in the name of the Lord. *This prayer, made in faith, will heal the sick man; the Lord will restore him to health . . . ." (James 5:14-15)

Anointing is not only for the dying. It is for any Catholic who "begins to be in danger of death from sickness or old age." These people should receive the sacrament to gain strength in body and soul.

The Twelve anointed sick people with oil and healed them (Mark 6:13). This practice became the Anointing sacrament of James chapter 5.

"Jesus went all over Galilee . . . healing people from every kind of disease and sickness . . . Jesus healed them all." (Matthew 4:23-24)

When someone in your family should be anointed, call Father at the church rectory. Father will set a time to come to your home. Be ready for the Anointing. Cover a small table with a cloth. Put a crucifix and two lighted candles on the table. If you have it, put holy water on the table with a dish and two pieces of cotton. To help the sick person to swallow Holy Communion, put out a glass of water and a spoon. When Father arrives, meet him at the door with a lighted candle.

41 How is marriage a covenant?
(Permanent, exclusive sharing)

A man and a woman get married because they love each other very much. They want to be together for life. At their wedding, the priest says to them:

Will you honor each other as man and wife for the rest of your lives? Will you accept children lovingly from God, and bring them up according to the law of Christ and his Church?

The man and the woman say to each other:

I take you to be my husband/my wife. I promise to be true to you in good times and in bad, in sickness and in health. I will love you and honor you all the days of my life.

At their wedding, the husband and wife make a *loving commitment*. They promise to live for each other. All their lives they will help each other. If anything goes wrong, they will forgive each other. They will share fun and happiness. They will share work and problems. They will share faith in Jesus with each other and with their children. Sharing their lives — this is what marriage is all about. It is a loving covenant.

God has a covenant with His people. Jesus has a covenant with His Church. The married couple have a covenant too. Their marriage is *permanent*: it is for the rest of their lives. Their marriage is *exclusive*: they will not love anyone else as husband or wife. Their love for each other shows everyone how much Jesus loves His covenant people.

Read Genesis 1:27-28,31 – God made man and woman "in the image of himself," intending that they live together and have children.

Read Genesis 2:24 and Matthew 19:3-6 – two in one flesh.

Read what the Second Vatican Council says about marriage and family (Church in the Modern World, 47 through 52).

42 Why do people become priests?
(Holy Orders; Role of clergy)

Think of your favorite priest. Do you know how he got to be a priest? The answer is: he became a priest through the sacrament of HOLY ORDERS.

People who receive Holy Orders have a special calling from God. If a person really *wants* to be a priest, God may be calling that person in a special way.

As His Body, all of Christ's faithful share in His priesthood. There is also the ministerial priesthood of Holy Orders which empowers the ordained to act "in the person of Christ the Head" (Vatican Council II, Ministry and Life of Priests, 2).

Though "marked with a special character" which unites them in a sacramental bond with one another, ordained priests "deal with other men as brothers" just as Jesus did (Vatican Council II, Ministry and Life of Priests, 2).

People who are going to be priests go to a special school. This school is called a seminary. At the seminary, future priests learn to be leaders of God's people. In medical school, future doctors learn to care for people's bodies. In the seminary, future priests learn to care for the Body of Jesus, His people. Future priests learn to pray so they can help other people to pray. They learn about the Bible so they can teach the Bible to other people. They learn about the Commandments and the Beatitudes, the Mass and the sacraments. They learn to follow Jesus so they can lead other people to follow Jesus.

Priests have a very important mission in life. Their mission is to help us love one another. Their mission is to help us forgive one another. Their mission is to help us become a closer, more loving Body of Jesus.

Jesus is our High Priest. In the Bible, the Book of Hebrews says: "Jesus is the High Priest who meets our needs . . . He offered one sacrifice, once and for all, when he offered himself." (Hebrews 7:26,27) Priests who receive Holy Orders help us to follow Jesus, our High Priest.

43 What are the parts of the Mass? (Liturgy of Word, Eucharist)

The Eucharistic Liturgy is called Holy Mass. Here are the different parts of the Mass.

LITURGY OF THE WORD — THE FIRST PART OF THE MASS

The Mass begins with a song and opening prayers. Then *God speaks to you* in the liturgy of the WORD.

- THE FIRST READING is the Word of God from the Old Testament. After this Word, you respond to God with a Psalm.
- THE SECOND READING, on Sundays, is usually from a Letter of Saint Paul. After this Word, you respond with an "Alleluia" or a chant that helps you want to hear the Gospel reading.
- THE GOSPEL READING is from Matthew, Mark, Luke, or John. This is God's Word to you from the life of Jesus Himself.
- THE HOMILY is the word of God from your priest or deacon. When you listen to the homily with great care, you hear how you can *keep* and *obey* God's Word to you. (Luke 11:28)
- THE PROFESSION OF FAITH is your "Yes" of faith to the whole liturgy of the Word. This prayer of faith is called the Nicene Creed.
- THE PRAYER OF THE FAITHFUL is the final part in the liturgy of the Word. Prayers are said, asking God to help people.

Chapter 6 of Saint John's Gospel portrays Jesus as Word and Eucharist. The Jerusalem Bible comments: "Jesus is the true bread because he is God's Word, verses 32f, and also because he is a victim whose body and blood are offered in sacrifice for the life of the world, verses 51-58."

LITURGY OF THE EUCHARIST — THE SECOND PART OF THE MASS

After the WORD comes the EUCHARIST. *Eucharist* means "giving thanks." You respond to the liturgy of the WORD with the liturgy of THANKS. You remember Jesus, you sacrifice with Him, and you share His holy meal.

- **THE PREPARATION OF THE GIFTS** comes first. It begins as bread, wine, and water are brought to the altar. These gifts will become the body and blood of Jesus. This is also the time when money or other gifts are collected for the poor and the Church. The priest prays over the gifts, asking the Father to accept and bless them. Jesus offers Himself and His Body to the Father. You and everyone here are His Body. Jesus is offering *you* to the Father. Tell the Father what you want to offer Him. Offer your work today. Offer the things you like, and the things you do not like. Offer yourself with Jesus.

- **THE EUCHARISTIC PRAYER** comes next. This is the high point of the Mass. It begins with the Preface, a prayer of thanksgiving. At the end of the Preface, you say or sing the "Holy, Holy, Holy." The Eucharistic Prayer has several parts. *To learn these parts, open a missal or missalette. Find Eucharistic Prayer IV.* Here are its different parts:

  1. *Praise to the Father.* This part begins with "Father, we acknowledge your greatness" and ends with "bring us the fullness of grace."

The "Holy, Holy, Holy" has its roots in Isaiah 6:3.

2. *Prayer for the Spirit.* This part begins with "Father, may this Holy Spirit" and ends with "everlasting covenant." In this prayer, the Church asks the Father to send the Spirit. The Spirit makes your offerings holy. The Spirit makes them the body and blood of Jesus.

3. *The Last Supper.* This part begins with "He always loved" and ends with "Do this in memory of me." Here and now, Jesus speaks through His priest. He says: *"Take this, all of you . . . this is my body . . . this is my blood."* The bread and wine have now become His body and blood. His Passover from death to Life is now here in your midst.

4. *Response.* In this Mass, the risen Jesus has brought His sacrifice to you at this altar. The priest invites everyone to *respond* to this wonderful happening. He says: "Let us proclaim the mystery of faith." One of the responses you may say is: *"Christ has died, Christ is risen, Christ will come again."*

5. *Memorial prayer.* This part begins with "Father, we now celebrate" and ends with "salvation to the whole world." In this part you *remember* the past: Jesus dying and rising. You *remember* the future: that day at the end of time when Jesus will come in glory. On that day, His kingdom will come and make the whole world new. From that day on, we will live in "a kingdom of justice, love, and peace."

Prayer 2 on this page is called the epiclesis *(ep-e-CLE-sis). The word means a "calling upon." The Holy Spirit is called to change bread and wine into the body and blood of Jesus.*

Prayer 5 on this page is called the anamnesis *(an-am-NE-sis). The word means "memorial" or "remembering."*

6. *Prayer for the Spirit.* This part begins with "Lord, look" and ends with "sacrifice of praise." Here you ask that the Spirit may "gather all who share this bread and wine into the one body of Christ."

7. *Prayer for the Church.* This part begins with "Lord, remember" and ends with "a sincere heart." This is a prayer for the Pope, for your Bishop, and for all of God's people.

8. *Prayer for the dead.* This part begins with "Remember those" and ends with "you alone." This is a prayer for all who have died.

9. *Prayer for union with the saints.* This part begins with "Father, in your mercy" and ends with "everything that is good." Here you pray that all of us will join Mary, the Apostles, and all the saints in heaven.

10. *Hymn of praise.* This part begins with "Through him" and ends with your response: "Amen." This is the final part of the Eucharistic Prayer. Your "Amen" here is your great "Yes" to Jesus. You are saying, "YES, Jesus, I am offering myself with You to our Father. All glory and honor is yours, almighty Father, for ever and ever."

- THE COMMUNION RITE is the third and final part of the liturgy of the Eucharist. To prepare for Holy Communion, everyone together prays the *Our Father*. When you say "our daily bread" in the Our Father, let these words remind you of Jesus, the Bread of Life.

Next, the priest invites everyone to share a *sign of peace*. You may give the sign of peace by turning to your neighbor and saying, "The peace of Christ be with you." You may want to use other words. You may want to shake hands. The important thing is to make this a true sign. With this sign, you are saying: "We are His Body. We share His peace."

Next, the priest breaks the bread — the sacred Host. He drops a piece of the Host into the cup — the chalice. Let this "breaking of bread" remind you of the Stranger at Emmaus — Luke 24:30,35. The risen Jesus is here with you now. During the breaking of bread, everyone says or sings the "Lamb of God."

The priest now holds up the sacred Host. He says: "Behold the Lamb of God . . . ." You respond: "Lord, I am not worthy to receive you, but only say the word and I shall be healed." Remember Zacchaeus — Luke 19:1-10. Jesus came to Zacchaeus' home and had supper with him. This healed Zacchaeus — he now felt worthy to be a part of Jesus' family. By coming to you in Holy Communion, Jesus heals you. When you sin, you hurt yourself. In Holy Communion, Jesus heals you by helping you to love people you have hurt. He heals you by helping you to forgive people who have hurt you.

In ancient times, the sign of peace took place at every Eucharistic celebration. Saint Paul witnesses to this custom in the earliest New Testament writings – 1 Thessalonians 5:26; 1 Corinthians 16:20.

Now it is time for Holy Communion. The person who gives you the sacred Host says, *"The body of Christ."* You respond: *"Amen."* You may receive the Host on your tongue, if you wish. If it is allowed, you may receive the Host in your hand. You then put it on your tongue and swallow it.

(Sometimes Holy Communion is also given from the cup. When this is done, the person holding the cup says, *"The blood of Christ."* You respond: *"Amen."* Take the cup slowly in both hands. Take a sip from the cup. Then give the cup back to the person who gave it to you.)

When you say *"Amen,"* this is what you are saying: "Yes, Lord, this is Your risen body. Yes, Lord, we are Your Body the Church."

After you have received, talk to Jesus in your heart. Thank Him for being with you. Ask Him to help you love His Body — your family, your fellow Catholics, all people on earth and in heaven.

If there is singing during this time, sing with everyone. This is how the Family celebrates.

The priest brings the liturgy of the Eucharist to a close with the Prayer after Communion. The Mass ends when the priest blesses everyone and says, "The Mass is ended . . . go in peace to love and serve the Lord." You respond by saying, "Thanks be to God." Your great prayer of thanks — Eucharist — has ended. Now you serve the Lord by serving and helping others.

Receiving the sacred Host in the hand, palms up, and saying "Amen" was common custom in earlier centuries.

44 How can Sunday Mass help your family? (Family at Eucharist)

Sunday Mass is Family Time. Whenever you can, go to Sunday Mass with your parents and relatives. Sunday Mass can bring your family closer together. Here are some ways you can help this to happen:

- At the beginning of Mass the priest says: "My brothers and sisters... let us call to mind our sins." Try to remember: *Have I hurt anyone in my family during the past week?* Ask for forgiveness in your heart. Ask yourself: *Has anyone in my family hurt me?* Forgive that person in your heart.

- At the Preparation of the Gifts, think of each person in your family. Think of the ways you help each person. Helping is hard work. It is sacrifice. Our Father loves your sacrifices for the family. Offer these sacrifices with Jesus.

- At the Sign of Peace, think of your family. Give family members a *special* sign of peace. Give them a hug. Smile. Be happy you are together. Say: "Thanks for helping me." Say: "Let's be friends." Say: "I love you."

- When you receive Holy Communion, you say: "Amen." (Yes, Lord, we are Your Body, the Church.) Your family is the Church, too. Jesus is in each person you live with. When you look at your family, you are looking at Jesus. Think of them when you receive Holy Communion.

According to Saint Augustine, the "Amen" we say at Holy Communion stands for the threefold body of Christ: His risen body, His Body the Church, and His Eucharistic body. Our "Amen" means: "Yes, we are the body of Christ."

Workshop

Words to Know

- COMMITMENT: a strong decision and promise to act or live in a certain, definite way.
- RECONCILIATION: the restoring of friendship; becoming friends again. The sacrament of Penance is called Reconciliation to show that God's loving forgiveness brings us closer to Him, to show that our heartfelt praise of His mercy makes us loving and closer to one another.
- PRIEST: a person whose Holy Orders give the ability to celebrate Holy Mass, to forgive sins in the sacrament of Reconciliation. Priests do not have the ability to ordain other priests; only Bishops can ordain.
- DEACON: a person whose Holy Orders give the ability to preach and teach the Word of God, to distribute the Holy Eucharist, to baptize and to be the Church's official witness at the sacrament of Matrimony. Deacons do not celebrate Mass or forgive sins in the sacrament of Reconciliation.

Mini-test

1. What is the definition of a sacrament that your parents learned as children? (Page 53)
2. Name the seven sacraments. (Page 53)
3. Why is a sacrament a meeting with Jesus? (Page 53)
4. What do all seven sacraments do? (Page 53)
5. Why is Baptism a sacrament of initiation? Why is Confirmation? Why is Eucharist? (Page 54)
6. Why does the Holy Eucharist remind you of manna in the desert? (Pages 54 and 15)
7. Why is Reconciliation a sacrament of healing? Why is Anointing of the Sick? (Page 54)
8. What do married people promise? What do Bishops, priests, and deacons promise? (Page 54)

9. How does Baptism free you from sin? How does it give you a new birth? How does it make you a member of God's Church? (Page 55)
10. How does Confirmation change you? (Page 56)
11. What makes the bread of Holy Eucharist so special? (Page 57)
12. What does our sharing of the "one bread" do for Jesus' Body the Church? (Page 57)
13. What four things do you do in Reconciliation with Jesus and His priest? (Page 58)
14. What are the steps you follow when you go to confession? (Page 59)
15. What does Anointing do for old or sick people who are not going to die soon? What does Anointing do for persons who may die soon? (Page 60)
16. How do you prepare at home for the sacrament of Anointing? (Page 60)
17. What do a husband and wife promise at their wedding? (Page 61)
18. The sacrament of Matrimony is permanent and exclusive. What does "permanent" mean? What does "exclusive" mean? (Page 61)
19. How do people who want to become priests prepare for Holy Orders? (Page 62)
20. What is a priest's mission in life? (Page 62)
21. What are the main parts in the Liturgy of the Word? (Page 63)
22. What does the word *Eucharist* mean? (Page 64)
23. What takes place during the Preparation of the Gifts? (Page 64)
24. In a missal or missalette, locate the ten parts of Eucharistic Prayer IV. (Pages 64-66)
25. How is your receiving Holy Communion like Zacchaeus being visited by Jesus? (Page 67)
26. What does "Amen" mean when you say it as you receive Holy Communion? (Page 68)
27. Name two ways Sunday Mass can help your family to become closer. (Page 69) What other things can you think of to do at Sunday Mass that will help your family to be closer?

Write and Share at Home

1. Write and tell what the word *sacrament* means to you.
2. Your journey through life is like the Hebrews' desert journey to the Promised Land. Which sacrament do you think helps you the most on your journey?
3. One of the early Church Fathers wrote: "My last name is Christian; my first name is Catholic." Tell what makes you happy to be a Catholic Christian.
4. What part of the Mass do you like best? Tell why.

Pray and Do

1. The Last Supper was the first Holy Mass. Read what Jesus did and said at the Last Supper in the Gospel of Saint John, chapter 13.
2. Memorize these words that you sometimes say in the Eucharistic Prayer at Mass. Use these words as a daily prayer.

   Lord, by your cross and resurrection you have set us free. You are the Savior of the world.

UNIT EIGHT: YOU LIVE BY JESUS' LAW OF LOVE

45 Why do people suffer?
(Original, personal sin; Salvation)

What would it be like if the world were perfect? There would be no more wars, no starving children. People would always help each other. The world would be like a great birthday party, full of love and happiness.

Do you know why the world is not perfect? There are two causes. The first cause is *original sin*. The Book of Genesis tells of Adam and Eve breaking their friendship with God. Because of original sin, there is much suffering in the world today.

Original sin makes us feel like being selfish. We do not *have to* do selfish things. We are free. We can choose to do loving things. If we choose to do selfish things, we commit *personal sin*. Personal sin is the second reason the world is not perfect.

When we sin, we say "No" to God our Father. When we know what God wants, but say "No," that is a sin. Every sin, large or small, hurts someone. Every sin adds to the suffering in the world.

There is much evil in the world. Every day thousands of poor people die of hunger. Innocent people are killed in wars. These evils are caused by original sin and personal sin.

Sin is bad news. But there is also Good News. The Good News is: Jesus is with us. His dying and rising have saved us from sin. At the end of time, Jesus will "make all things new!" The Bible says: "He will wipe away all tears from their eyes. There will be no more death, no more grief, crying, or pain." (Revelation 21:5,4)

Sharing the Light of Faith (the National Catechetical Directory for Catholics of the United States) says that "the root cause of social injustice, selfishness, and violence resides within the human person: the imbalances of the modern world are linked to a more basic imbalance in the human heart. Injustice, greed, lack of mercy, violence, and war are social consequences of sin" (NCD, 170).

46 What is a personal sin?
(Types, conditions for personal sin)

Do you remember the story of the son who left home? (Luke 15:11-32) We are all a little like that son. If we commit a really serious (mortal) sin, it is like leaving our home and Father. If we commit a lesser (venial) sin, we do not leave home. But we are not as close to our Father as before. Even small venial sins are bad news.

If a person *really wants* to do something that he *knows* is *very bad*, that could be a mortal sin. In case of a mortal sin, the ordinary way to return to the Father's love is to go to confession to a priest. No one *has to* go to confession unless he is *sure* there was a mortal sin.

A person can sin by *committing* or *doing* something wrong (a sin of commission). A person can sin by *omitting* or *not* doing something he should do (a sin of omission). A person can sin by *enjoying an evil thought*. (An example would be: enjoying the thought that someone we do not like had a bad accident.) A person can sin by *desiring* to do something, even if he does not do it. (An example would be: desiring to steal some money, but being unable to find it.)

Suppose a mother tells her three-year-old child to do something. The child hears his mother, but right away he forgets. Did he disobey his mother? No — because he did not *mean* to. He just forgot. Little children do all kinds of things they do not mean to do. So do older children and adults. Sin is always *on purpose*. It is always *deliberate*. If we do something we did not *mean* to do, it is not a sin.

Jesus' most important words about sin and virtue are found in the Sermon on the Mount – Matthew chapters 5, 6, and 7. Jesus looks at our outward way of life, but He also looks at our inner attitudes. Read Matthew 5:20.

Read Matthew 5:21-26 – about anger.
Read Matthew 5:38-42 – about revenge.
Read Matthew 5:43-48 – about love for enemies.
Read Matthew 6:1-4 – about charity.
Read Matthew 7:1-5 – about judging others.

47 How do you die to sin?
(Conversion; Family; Reconciliation)

In the Eucharistic Prayer, you say to Jesus: *Dying you destroyed our death, rising you restored our life. Lord Jesus, come in glory.*

As a baptized member of Jesus' Body, you have "died to sin." You live His new, risen Life. But traces of original sin remain. You still feel like being selfish. You need to keep being "converted" to God.

Conversion is very hard work. It is a job that lasts all your life. But remember this: GOD does the converting. You cannot convert yourself. Your job is to *keep trying*. Keep doing your best. Then, *let God take care of everything*. When you do your best, God is converting you.

Conversion to God is always needed because its opposite is always present. Read Romans 7:14-25.

Conversion is a family matter. You die to selfishness at home. You do this by helping each other — by praying together — by forgiving each other— by sharing Eucharist together. When you live this way, God is converting your family. You are dying to sin. Jesus is living His risen Life in your home.

Sometimes you may feel, "I am no good." You may think that all you do is make mistakes. You try, but nothing good happens. No one understands you. Maybe you feel that way after a fight at home, or when you get in trouble. This is a good time for the sacrament of Reconciliation. Go and tell your story to an understanding priest. Let Jesus heal you. Let him give you a new start. Reconciliation is a great help for conversion.

Conversion is in the heart: "I will give them a heart to know that I am the Lord . . . they shall return to me with their whole heart." (Jeremiah 24:7)

48 How does God ask you to love?
(Conscience; Decision-making)

What would it be like if you lived alone on an island? There would be no one around to tell you what to do. You would be your own boss. Would you like that?

In a way, you already *are* your own boss. The only person who can make you really want something is *you*. Even God does not make you do anything. God *asks* you. God *invites* you to love. God calls to you in your *conscience*.

You know God's Ten Commandments. You know Jesus' two great Commandments of Love. But sometimes you have to make a decision. You have to ask yourself: *Should I do this or not?* Sometimes you know right away: *This is what I should do. This is how Jesus wants me to love.* But sometimes it is not that simple. Sometimes you must pray and ask: *Lord, what are You asking me to do?* When you are trying to make up your mind in this way, your conscience is at work. You are "alone with God" in the "most secret core" of your heart.

The Second Vatican Council speaks of conscience in the following places: The Church, articles 8 and 16; Religious Freedom, articles 1, 2, and 3.

You know God's Law of Love. You are free to choose. You can choose to love. You can choose to sin. It is your decision. It is your responsibility. It is your conscience.

God gives you many helps when you have to make a decision. You can pray to the Holy Spirit in your heart. You can talk to family members. You can go to your priests and teachers. In your conscience you are alone with God. But others can help you to answer the question: *Lord, what are You asking me to do?*

49 When is your conscience Christian? (The Beatitudes)

Jesus wants you to keep the Ten Commandments. He wants you to keep them with His own attitudes. The attitudes of Jesus are called "Beatitudes." When you live by Jesus' Beatitudes, you are keeping His Law of Love. When you live by Jesus' Beatitudes, you are happy. Here are the eight Beatitudes from the Gospel of Saint Matthew:

HAPPY are those who know they are spiritually poor; the kingdom of heaven belongs to them!
You are poor in spirit if . . .

- You know that having things your way cannot make you happy.
- You know that being totally independent cannot make you happy.
- You know that having money cannot make you happy.
- You really trust God your Father to take care of you.
- You let people help you when you need help.
- You trust God to take care of your family and loved ones.
- You say and really mean: "Father! In Your hands I place my spirit!" (Luke 23:46)

HAPPY are those who mourn; God will comfort them!
To mourn means to be sorry about something. You "mourn" with Jesus when . . .

- You are sorry that you sometimes hurt others.
- You are sorry that you do not always help others.
- You are sorry that you do not always try to make your family members happy.
- You are sorry that some people do not love God with all their heart.
- You are sorry that sin causes many people in this world to suffer and die.
- You are sorry that some people do not know that God loves them with all His heart.

Jesus' Beatitudes are prophetic sayings. Jesus sides with the poor and the oppressed; He promises them freedom and happiness. Jesus clearly condemns the oppressive use of wealth and power; read Luke 6:24-26.

HAPPY are those whose greatest desire is to do what God requires; God will satisfy them fully! What God "requires" means "God's will for you." You greatly desire to do what God requires when . . .

- You tell the Father every day: "Thy will be done."
- You really believe that whatever you say or do to any person, you say or do to Jesus.
- You pray for the grace to be forgiving at home.
- You are determined to help others whenever you can.
- You really want to grow closer to our Lord. You really want Him to convert you.

HAPPY are the meek; they will receive what God has promised! To be meek means to be *strong* in a very *gentle* way. You are meek if . . .

- You keep calm when you are treated unfairly.
- You say no in a kind way when you are invited to do something that is wrong.
- You are kind to people in your family when they irritate you.
- You say "I'm sorry" when you have hurt someone.
- You do not fight back when someone picks a fight with you.
- You do kind things for people even when you know they will not thank you.

Mary's Magnificat (Luke 1:46-55) expresses some of the same strong views found in the Beatitudes.

HAPPY are those who are merciful to others; God will be merciful to them!

To be merciful means to be very kind and very forgiving. You are merciful to others when . . .

- You know that every person you see has feelings just as you do.
- You try never to *judge* another person. You do not know for sure that anyone means to sin. God knows, and God is forgiving.
- You forgive the same person over and over again — because God forgives you over and over.
- You keep from showing anger when someone bothers you.
- You are kind to people who are not kind to you.

HAPPY are the pure in heart; they will see God!

To be pure in heart means that you do not want anything that goes against God's law. You want only what God wants. You are pure in heart if . . .

- You do not want to go against any of the Ten Commandments. (Review the Ten Commandments on page 16 of this book.)
- You stay away from anyone who can get you to do things that are wrong.
- You want every person you know to be happy.
- You love God so much that you want to help and forgive everyone — especially the members of your own family.

Jesus was delivering a serious, prophetic message when He said things such as Luke 16:19-23 and Mark 12:41-44, and acted as in Mark 11:15-19 and Luke 19:1-10.

Lord, make me a channel of your peace.

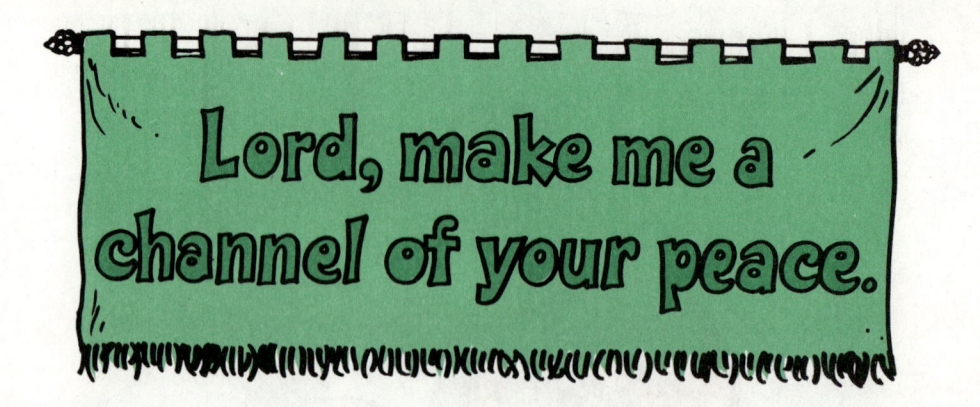

HAPPY are those who work for peace among men; God will call them his sons!
To "work for peace" means to help people love each other when they do not get along together. You work for peace when . . .

- You do anything you can to keep people from fighting.
- You say: "Why don't you shake hands and be friends?"
- You say: "Let's stop fighting and be friends."
- You tell your relative or friend that you feel bad that he or she is fighting with a person you love.
- You pray for relatives or friends who are angry or fighting with each other.

HAPPY are those who are persecuted because they do what God requires; the Kingdom of heaven belongs to them!
Some people do not understand Jesus. Some people do not like Jesus' followers. These people hurt Jesus' friends and make them suffer. You are "persecuted" for Jesus when . . .

- Others get angry with you because you refuse to break the law of God.
- Others think you are strange because you follow your religion.
- You remember the words of Jesus on the Cross: "Father, forgive them! They don't know what they are doing." (Luke 23:34)

Memorize the Beatitudes. Think of them daily when you pray the Our Father. Think of them when you are trying to do God's will. When the Beatitudes of Jesus guide your conscience, you are living as a true Christian.

The Jewish elite realized very well that Jesus meant what He was saying, and that He was talking about them. Read Matthew 21:45 and 46; Mark 12:12. This is why they decided to get rid of Him; read Luke 20:19 and 20.

50 What are some signs of a true Christian? (Works of Mercy)

*What good is it for someone to say, "I have faith,"
if his actions do not prove it?*
— SAINT JAMES 2:14

*To be truly Catholic is . . . above all to be able to enter
into the problems and joys of all,
to understand all, to be all things to all men.*
— FATHER THOMAS MERTON

You will know them by their deeds.
— THE LORD JESUS

The Bodily Works of Mercy
1. Feed the hungry.
2. Give drink to the thirsty.
3. Clothe the naked.
4. Visit the imprisoned.
5. Shelter the homeless.
6. Visit the sick.
7. Bury the dead.

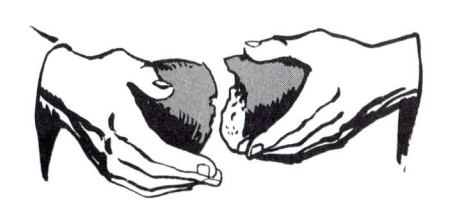

The Spiritual Works of Mercy
1. Correct those who do harm.
2. Teach the ignorant.
3. Counsel those who need advice.
4. Comfort those who suffer.
5. Be patient with others.
6. Forgive those who hurt you.
7. Pray for all, living and dead.

51 What Catholic duties help you to love? (Precepts of the Church)

As a Christian, you live by the Commandments, the Beatitudes, and the Works of Mercy. As a CATHOLIC Christian, you are guided also by Church teaching. Here are some of the duties that help Catholics to love God and neighbor.

1. To worship God by taking part in the Mass every Sunday and holy day of obligation; to avoid unnecessary work on these days.

2. To receive Holy Communion often and the sacrament of Reconciliation regularly. Holy Communion should be received at least once a year, between the first Sunday of Lent and Trinity Sunday. The sacrament of Reconciliation must be received once a year only if serious sin is involved.

3. To study Catholic teaching in preparation for the sacrament of Confirmation; to be confirmed; to continue to study and advance the cause of Christ.

4. To observe the marriage laws of the Church; to give religious training, by example and word, to one's children; to use parish schools and catechetical programs.

5. To strengthen and support the Church — one's own parish community and parish priests, the worldwide Church, and our Holy Father the Pope.

6. To do penance — which includes abstaining from meat and fasting from food — on the appointed days.

7. To join in the missionary spirit and apostolate of the Church.

Earlier in this century there was a list of six duties for Catholics called the Precepts of the Church. The list on this page does not have such a title. The present list incorporates the duties found in the Precepts. Numbers 3 and 7 in the present list were not among the Precepts.

Workshop

Words to Know

- ORIGINAL SIN: The Second Vatican Council says the following about the Fall and original sin: "Although he was made by God in a state of holiness, from the very dawn of history man abused his liberty, at the urging of personified Evil. Man set himself against God and sought to find fulfillment apart from God . . . he became out of harmony with himself, with others, and with all created things. Therefore man is split within himself . . . Indeed, man finds that by himself he is incapable of battling the assaults of evil successfully, so that everyone feels as though he is bound by chains." (Church in the Modern World, 13)
- PERSONAL SIN: a deliberate breaking of God's law by desire, decision, word, act, or omission.
- CONVERSION: a turning to God. The most basic conversion a person can undergo is from the state of being *away from* God (the state of sin) to being *with* God (the state of grace). In grace, God constantly calls us to deeper repentance and conversion, deeper love for Him and for His people. A new stage of conversion sometimes comes through a religious experience. (The term *conversion* is also used to mean changing one's religion — e.g., conversion to the Catholic Church.)
- CONSCIENCE: The Second Vatican Council says the following about conscience: "In the depths of his conscience, man detects a law which he does not impose upon himself, but which holds him to obedience. Always summoning him to love good and avoid evil, the voice of conscience can when necessary speak to his heart more specifically: do this, shun that. For man has in his heart a law written by God. To obey it is the very dignity of man; according to it he will be judged." (Church in the Modern World, 16)
- BEATITUDES: statements of the paradoxical happiness of those who seek the salvation Jesus brings. In the Gospel of Matthew there are eight Beatitudes (5:3-10, with 5:11 as a further expression of 5:10). In the Gospel of Luke there are four Beatitudes (6:20-22, with 6:24-26 as contrasting woes or laments).
- KINGDOM OF HEAVEN: the reign or kingdom of God. The coming of God's kingdom was the heart of Jesus' message, and Jesus is the person through whom God is establishing His reign in our midst. The gradual process of God's reign coming among us is described in Vatican Council II, Church in the Modern World, 39.

Mini-test

1. Why do people suffer? (Page 73)
2. What is the difference between venial and mortal sin? (Page 74)
3. What are some ways a person can sin besides actually *doing* something wrong? (Page 74)
4. A personal sin is always deliberate. What does deliberate mean? (Page 74)
5. What does "being converted" mean? (Pages 75 and 83)
6. How can the sacrament of Reconciliation help you to keep being converted? (Page 75)
7. What does "conscience" mean? (Pages 76 and 83)
8. Recite the eight Beatitudes from the Gospel of Saint Matthew. Give an example of each Beatitude. (Pages 77-80)
9. Why is it important to do Works of Mercy? Recite the Bodily Works of Mercy. Recite the Spiritual Works of Mercy. (Page 81)
10. Recite the seven duties that help Catholics to love God and others. (Page 82)

Write and Share at Home

1. Give examples of how God is converting your family through the way family members live together. Find an example for each member of the family.
2. Give examples of Beatitudes your family members live by. Find an example for each member of the family.
3. Give examples of Works of Mercy your family members do. Find an example for each member of the family.

Pray and Do

1. Choose one of the Beatitudes that you will think of when you pray the Our Father every day.
2. Choose a Work of Mercy that you will do within the next week. If possible, choose a person, a time, and a place.

UNIT NINE: YOU LIVE WITH MARY AND THE SAINTS

52 What should you know about Mary? (Marian teaching)

Here are some things to remember about your mother, Mary.

When Mary was a young woman, an angel told her: "You are to have a son named Jesus." Mary's son, Jesus, is the Son of God. He did not have a human father. Mary, Jesus' mother, is the *Virgin Mother of God*.

The Father wanted His Son, Jesus, to have a very special mother. So God made Mary free from original sin. This is called her *Immaculate Conception*. Mary was not the least bit selfish. She never committed a single sin in her whole life.

After Jesus ascended into heaven, Mary wanted to be with Him. God now did a very special thing. God took Mary to heaven. Even her body went to heaven as a risen body. This is called Mary's *Assumption*. Mary is now risen. She is with Jesus.

Mary gave birth to Jesus as a baby. She stood near Him when He was dying on the Cross. She is now the Mother of His Body, the Church. Mary is *your* Mother. She is always thinking of you. When you talk to Mary, she listens to you. She loves you very much.

Mary is your great model of faith and love. Mary always kept the Word of God. She always followed the Holy Spirit. Pray to her every day. She is your mother. She is preparing a place for you in heaven.

The NCD, Sharing the Light of Faith, says about Mary: "The special love and veneration due her as mother of Christ, mother of the Church, and our spiritual mother should be taught by word and example" (NCD, 106).

The teaching of the Second Vatican Council about Mary is found in The Church, articles 52 through 69.

53 How can you show Mary you love her? (Prayers to Mary)

Here are some prayers to Mary.
Say these prayers with your family or your class.

Prayer to Be Good Christians

Dear Mother, * we love you because you are the Mother of Jesus and our Mother too. * Please ask your Son, Jesus, * for all the help we need * to be good Christians and Catholics.

Prayer for Ourselves

O Mary, * you are the mother of Jesus. * Please ask Him to help us live good lives, * help us avoid anger and disobedience, * lying and cheating, * at home and at school. * Help us to be sorry for our sins. * Help us to love others as you love us. * Keep us holy today and every day, * so that we will one day be with Jesus and you in heaven. * Pray for us now and at the hour of our death. Amen.

Prayer of Thanksgiving

Jesus, our Brother, * we thank you for sharing your Mother Mary with us. * Mary, we thank you for being our Mother. * We thank you for all the favors you have obtained * for us, * for our parents, * and for our friends. * To show our thanks, * we will try to live a good life, * and to praise God with you forever.

54 Who is a saint?
(Saints; Communion of Saints)

The word *saint* means "holy." A saint is a person who shares God's Life of grace. A saint is a person who loves God and others.

There are many living saints. Some saints are so wonderful that their lives become famous. After they die, the Church canonizes them. The Church says: "This person is a saint in heaven. Try to love God and others as much as this person did. Pray to this saint."

There are saints in heaven and saints on earth. Everyone in heaven is a saint. All of your relatives in heaven are saints. If you pray to your relatives in heaven, they will hear you and help you. People on earth can talk to people in heaven. People in heaven can help people on earth. We are like one big family. This family is called *the Communion of Saints*. The word *Communion* means being-together-in-love. At Holy Communion time, you are together in love with Jesus. In the Communion of Saints, you are always together with all the saints in heaven and on earth.

This is My Body...

Are you named after a saint? Did you get a saint's name at Confirmation? Whatever your saint's name is, get in touch with your saint. Talk to your saint and ask for help. Read about your saint. Learn how you can love others the way your saint did on earth. Your saint in heaven can help you to grow in love.

Of all the people who ever lived, Mary is the greatest saint. Of course, Mary takes second place to Jesus. He is the Son of God. At Mass we tell Jesus: "You alone are the Holy One."

The teaching of the Second Vatican Council about the saints and the Communion of Saints is found in The Church, articles 49 through 51.

Workshop

Words to Know

- **IMMACULATE CONCEPTION:** On December 8, 1854, Pope Pius IX defined the doctrine of the Immaculate Conception. The Pope said that Mary "in the first instant of her conception was, by a singular grace and privilege of Almighty God and because of the merits of Jesus Christ the Savior of the human race, free from all stain of original sin."
- **ASSUMPTION:** In 1950, Pope Pius XII defined the Assumption of Mary as a dogma of Catholic faith. This teaching says that Mary was "assumed," or taken up, bodily into heaven by the power of God. This teaching has always been believed in the Church, and has been celebrated as a feast for over 1,500 years. The feast of Mary's Assumption is August 15, a holy day of obligation.
- **MARY, MOTHER OF THE CHURCH:** Especially since the Second Vatican Council, Catholics look upon Mary as Mother of the Church. The Council says: "The Son whom she brought forth is He whom God placed as the first-born among many brethren (cf. Rom. 8:29), namely, the faithful. In their birth and development she cooperates with a maternal love." (*The Church*, 63)
- **CANONIZE:** A person is "canonized" a saint when the Pope declares that he or she is in heaven. In the canonization process, the person is first declared to be *Venerable*, then *Blessed*, and finally a *Saint*.
- **COMMUNION OF SAINTS:** The Communion of Saints is the bond of oneness that exists between the People of God on earth and those who have gone before us. Vatican Council II focuses on this bond of union by saying that it "accepts with great devotion the venerable faith of our ancestors regarding this vital fellowship with our brethren who are in heavenly glory or who are still being purified after death." (*The Church*, 51) In the section quoted, the Council points out that just as we on earth can help those "who are still being purified," those in heaven can help us on our journey through life by interceding with God.

Mini-test

1. Why is Mary called the Virgin Mother of God? (Page 85)
2. What does "Immaculate Conception" mean? (Pages 85 and 88)
3. What does "Assumption" mean? (Pages 85 and 88)
4. What does "saint" mean? (Page 87)
5. What is the Communion of Saints? (Pages 87 and 88)
6. Who is the greatest of the saints? (Page 87)

Write and Share at Home

1. Read about Mary at the foot of the Cross in the Gospel of Saint John, 19:25-27. If you were Mary watching Jesus die, how would you feel? What thoughts would go through your mind during those three hours?
2. Have each family member make a simple 8½ x 11 poster about his or her favorite saint. Besides a drawing of the saint, each poster should show the years of the saint's birth and death, the date of the saint's feast day, and a word or phrase describing the saint's outstanding quality or virtue. For example: Saint Monica — 322?-387 — Feast day: August 27 — Outstanding qualities: Patience and Prayer. (A good source for such information is SAINT OF THE DAY, two small paperback books which give "A Life and Lesson for Each of the 173 Saints of the New Missal." Volume 1 covers saints whose feasts are from January through June; Volume 2 covers July through December. SAINT OF THE DAY is published by St. Anthony Messenger Press.)

Pray and Do

1. Pray the prayers to Mary that you find on page 86 of this book.
2. Here is a prayer that your family can say at mealtime in honor of the day's saint.

Dear Father, help us, as we celebrate the memory of Saint N., to imitate his (her) way of life. May her (his) example challenge us to live holier lives. Grant this through our Lord Jesus Christ. Amen.

UNIT TEN: HOME IS WITH GOD

55 What happens when you die? (Judgment; Final destiny)

Once upon a time, you were a tiny baby in your mother's body. Even when you were that small, you had a human soul.

Some day you will die and go home to God. When you die, your soul will go out of your body. Your body will not move anymore. But you will be alive in your soul. You will be awake. You will know what is happening.

When you die, your *judgment* will take place. You will remember everything that ever happened in your life. You will see all the beautiful, loving things you did in your life. You will see all the love you received from God, from your family and friends. You will see how merciful God has been in forgiving your sins.

At the moment of judgment, you will know that you are going to heaven. If a person did not choose God at the moment of death, that person would not choose heaven as his home. That would be *hell* — separation from God forever. When you love God at the moment you die, you choose *heaven* as your home — happiness with God forever.

You may have some "stains of sin" when you die. Your soul may not be completely healed from sins you committed. You may still be a bit selfish. God takes away stains of sin by healing and purifying you. This purifying is called *purgatory*. After purgatory, you are able to love without any selfishness. You are filled with the Holy Spirit. You are in heaven.

The doctrine of resurrection from death had its beginnings in the Old Testament – read Isaiah, chapters 24-27 (esp. 26:9); 2 Maccabees 7:9, 7:14, 12:44. Jesus affirms resurrection of the body in Mark 12:16-27.

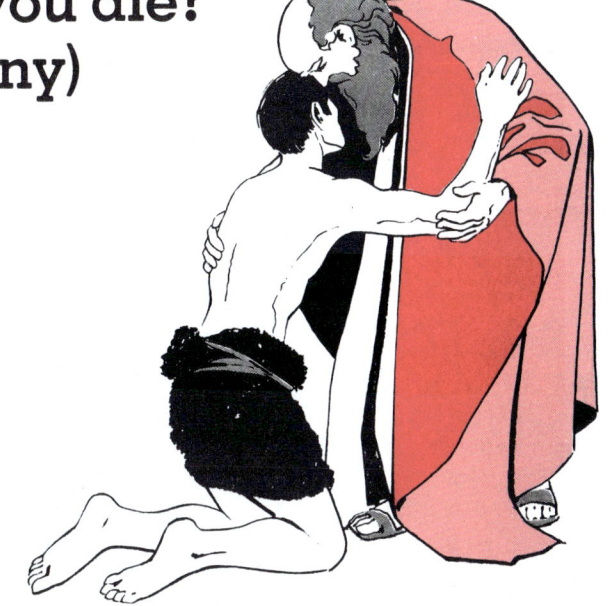

Concerning the human soul, the Council says: "When man recognizes in himself a spiritual and immortal soul, he is not being mocked by a deceptive fantasy springing from mere physical or social influences. On the contrary he is getting to the depths of the very truth of the matter" (Church in the Modern World, 14).

56 What will heaven be like?
(Happiness; Joy; Home at last)

God your Father loves you with His whole heart. He wants you to live with Him forever. When you go home to God, you will see Jesus and the Father face-to-face. You will be happier than anyone has ever been on earth.

In heaven you will be with Mary. All during your life Mary is waiting for you, praying for you. In heaven you will be able to see her and thank her. You will meet all your relatives who went to heaven before you. You will meet all the other saints who helped you during your life on earth.

Here on earth there is pain. Some pain comes from your body being hurt or sick. Some pain comes from being afraid or from having your feelings hurt. In heaven there is no pain of any kind. In heaven you will be alive with excitement and joy. You will be filled with the Holy Spirit. You will be with Jesus and the Father.

When you think of dying, think of heaven. Think of going home to God. Mother Teresa of Calcutta says: "To return to God is to return home." When you return to your Father, you will be home at last.

Sharing the Light of Faith speaks of "a life eternally with God beyond what the human heart can imagine, a life of eternal enjoyment of the good things God has prepared for those who love him" (NCD, 109).

57 What will happen when Jesus returns? (Judgment; New earth)

In the Eucharistic Prayer we say: *"When we eat this bread and drink this cup, we proclaim your death, Lord Jesus, until you come in glory."*

When will Jesus come in glory? We do not know. He may not come for ten thousand years. God has not told us when the Last Day will be. Many people have predicted the end of the world. All of these people have guessed wrong.

This we do know: when Jesus comes, there will be "the resurrection of the dead." You will see every person who ever lived. You will see Jesus. You will recognize Jesus in "the least important of these brothers" of His. Jesus will "judge the living and the dead."

On that Day Jesus will say: "And now I make all things new!" (Revelation 21:5) He will heal and purify our world. The world will become "a new earth where justice will abide." All the good dreams your parents have worked so hard for will come true.

Meanwhile, on this earth, God's kingdom "is already present in mystery. When the Lord returns, it will be brought into full flower."

What shall we do in this time before Jesus returns in glory? We shall look forward to His coming by sharing the Eucharistic bread. We shall work to make this a world of "human dignity, brotherhood, and freedom." We shall pray, in the words of the early Christians: COME, LORD JESUS!

Sharing the Light of Faith says: "The final realities will come about only when Christ returns with power to bring history to its appointed end. Then, as judge of the living and the dead, He will hand over His people to the Father. Only then will the Church reach perfection" (NCD, 110).

Workshop

Words to Know
- **JUDGMENT:** The Church believes in two final destinies — one for individuals, and one for humankind as a whole. Individual judgment at the instant of death consists in a crystal-clear revelation of one's unchangeable, freely chosen condition — eternal union with God, or eternal alienation.
- **PURGATORY:** The HANDBOOK FOR TODAY'S CATHOLIC states: "If you die in the love of God but possess any 'stains of sin,' such stains are cleansed away in a purifying process called purgatory. These stains of sin are primarily the temporal punishment due to venial or mortal sins already forgiven but for which sufficient penance was not done during your lifetime. This doctrine of purgatory, reflected in Scripture and developed in Tradition, was clearly expressed in the Second Council of Lyons (A.D. 1274). Having passed through purgatory, you will be utterly unselfish, capable of perfect love. Your selfish ego — that part of you that restlessly sought self-satisfaction — will have died forever. The 'new you' will be your same inner self, transformed and purified by the intensity of God's love for you."
- **HEAVEN:** In 1 Corinthians 13:12, Saint Paul says: "What I see now is like the dim image in a mirror; then we shall see face to face."

Mini-test
1. What will happen to you — to your soul — when you die? (Page 89)
2. When will your judgment take place? What will happen at your judgment? (Page 89)
3. What does purgatory mean? (Page 89)
4. What will heaven be like? (Page 90)
5. What does Mother Teresa of Calcutta say about dying? (Page 90)
6. When will Jesus come in glory? (Page 91)
7. What will happen when Jesus comes in glory? (Page 91; see also Vatican Council II, *Church in the Modern World*, 39)
8. What shall we do in this time before Jesus returns in glory? (Page 91)

Write and Share at Home
1. Tell what you look forward to most about going to heaven.
2. When Jesus makes "all things new" on the Last Day, all the good dreams your parents have worked for will come true. What are the good dreams your parents have worked for? What do you want the world to be like when Jesus renews it on the Last Day?

Pray and Do
Memorize and pray daily the Apostles' Creed.

I believe in God, the Father almighty, creator of heaven and earth; and in Jesus Christ, his only Son, our Lord; who was conceived by the Holy Spirit, born of the virgin Mary, suffered under Pontius Pilate, was crucified, died, and was buried. He descended to the dead; the third day he arose again from the dead; he ascended into heaven, sits at the right hand of God, the Father almighty; from thence he shall come to judge the living and the dead. I believe in the Holy Spirit, the Holy Catholic Church, the communion of saints, the forgiveness of sins, the resurrection of the body, and life everlasting. Amen.

Appendix A: Important Catholic Prayers

When you love someone, you want to talk to him or her. When you love God, you talk to Him. This is called praying.

Catholics pray to the Father, Son and Holy Spirit, and to Mary and the saints. The prayers you find listed here can help you to grow closer to God and to your family, the Church of Jesus.

1. The Sign of the Cross

In the name of the Father, and of the Son, and of the Holy Spirit. Amen. *(Said at the beginning and at the end of prayers.)*

2. The Our Father (The Lord's Prayer)

This prayer is found on page 26 of this book.

3. The Hail Mary

This prayer is found on page 32 of this book.

4. A Prayer of Praise (The Glory Be)

This prayer is found on page 38 of this book.

5. The Apostles' Creed

This prayer is found on page 92 of this book.

6. A Morning Offering

Almighty God, I thank You for Your past blessings. Today, I offer myself — whatever I do, say, or think — to Your loving care. Continue to bless me, Lord.

I make this morning offering in union with the divine intentions of Jesus Christ Who offers Himself daily in the holy Sacrifice of the Mass, and in union with Mary, His Virgin Mother and our Mother, who was always the faithful handmaid of the Lord.

(The acts of faith, hope, love, and contrition that follow are very good for morning and night prayers.)

7. An Act of Faith

O my God, I firmly believe that you are one God in three divine Persons, Father, Son, and Holy Spirit; I believe that your divine Son became man and died for our sins, and that He will come to judge the living and the dead. I believe these and all the truths which the Holy Catholic Church teaches, because You revealed them, Who can neither deceive nor be deceived.

8. An Act of Hope

O my God, relying on Your infinite goodness and promises, I hope to obtain pardon of my sins, the help of Your grace, and life everlasting, through the merits of Jesus Christ, my Lord and Redeemer.

9. An Act of Love

O my God, I love You above all things, with my whole heart and soul, because You are all good and worthy of all my love. I love my neighbor as myself for the love of You. I forgive all who have injured me and I ask pardon of all whom I have injured.

10. An Act of Contrition

My God, I am sorry for my sins with all my heart. In choosing to do wrong and failing to do good, I have sinned against You whom I should love above all things. I firmly intend, with Your help, to do penance, to sin no more, and to avoid whatever leads me to sin. Our Savior Jesus Christ suffered and died for us. In His name, my God, have mercy.

OR

O my God, I am sorry for my sins because I have offended You. I know I should love You above all things. Help me to do penance, to do better, and to avoid anything that might lead me to sin. Amen.

OR

Lord Jesus, Son of God, have mercy on me, a sinner.

11. Grace before Meals

From the heavens He sends down rain and rich harvests; our spirits He fills with food and delight.

Bless us, O Lord, and these Your gifts, which we are about to receive from Your goodness, through Christ, our Lord.

May the Lord provide for the needs of others and always be our heavenly food. Amen.

12. Grace after Meals

We give thanks for all Your benefits, almighty God, Who live and reign forever. May the souls of the faithful departed, through the mercy of God, rest in peace.

(It is also good to pray spontaneously, especially before meals.)

13. Mary's Rosary

This prayer is found on pages 47 and 48 of this book.

14. Hail, Holy Queen

This prayer is found on page 52 of this book.

Appendix B: An Examination of Conscience Based on the Commandments and the Words of Jesus

"Love the Lord your God" (Matthew 22:37).

1. Adore God alone.

- Do I love God with my whole heart, as His son or daughter?
- Do I do anything that keeps me from being close to God?
- Do I thank God for giving me family, friends, and food?
- Do I trust God as our Father who will one day bring us home to Him?

2. Respect God's holy name.

- Do I love Jesus, the Father's Word?
- Do I love the Church, the people of God's Word?
- Do I try to learn all I can about God, Jesus, and the Church?
- Do I always use God's name with love and respect?

- Do I respect the Father, Son, and Holy Spirit by seeing each person as the image of God, as a brother or sister of Jesus, as a person in whom the Holy Spirit is living?
- Do I show my love for God's Word by living it and sharing it with others?

3. Keep the Lord's day holy.

- Do I keep Sunday holy by taking part in Holy Mass with attention and devotion?
- Do I take part in Holy Mass on holy days of obligation?
- Do I receive Holy Communion often and the sacrament of Reconciliation regularly?
- Do I pray daily, trying to mean the words that I say?
- Do I try to make our world better, to get it ready for Jesus' coming on the Last Day?

"Love your fellowman as yourself" (Matthew 22:39).

4. Honor your parents and obey lawful authority.

- Do I always speak to my parents with respect?
- Do I honor my parents by obeying them?
- Do I help my parents by doing family jobs and by trying to make things easier for them?
- Do I do all I can to be loving and forgiving at home?
- Do I show love for myself and for others by obeying the rules of safety?
- Do I show love for others by obeying regulations at school and in public places?
- Do I have respect for people who exercise lawful authority?
- Am I bossy to anyone?
- Do I always do my homework from school? Do I give my parents all the notes my teachers send home?

5. Respect human life.

- Do I respect myself by remembering that the Father loves me with His whole heart?
- Do I respect myself by keeping clean and taking care of my health?
- Do I treat every person I meet with respect and kindness?
- Do I praise others when they deserve a compliment?
- When I can, do I help people who need help?
- Do I hurt anyone's feelings by criticizing? by name-calling?
- Do I annoy or pick on anyone?
- Do I hurt others by word or action if they make me angry?
- Do I look down on, or make fun of, poor people? handicapped people? elderly people? people of other races or nationalities?
- Do I hit, slap, shove, or fight with anyone?

6 and 9. Keep sex sacred.

- Do I respect my body as a wonderful gift from God?
- Do I say or do anything that goes against the sacredness of sex?
- Do I say or do anything that is indecent?

8. Respect the truth.

- Do I always tell the truth?
- Do I say things that I know are not true?
- Do I talk about others behind their backs?
- Do I get others in trouble by telling lies about them?
- Do I make promises that I do not keep?
- Do I cheat on tests or copy the work of others?

7 and 10. Respect the rights and property of others.

- Do I take things that are not mine?
- Do I take money that is not mine?
- Do I give away things and then take them back?
- Do I share my belongings with others?

Leader's Guide for How You Live with Jesus

If you teach religion in a Catholic school, or are a weekly CCD or PSR teacher, the Leader's Guide for this text can save you valuable class preparation time. A bridge between doctrinal content and real life, the Leader's Guide develops the all-important experiential dimension. Order the Leader's Guide, priced at $4.95, from your local bookstore. Or write Liguori Publications, Box 060, Liguori, Missouri 63057. (Please enclose 50¢ for postage and handling.)

Other helpful publications from the Redemptorists

For grades 4-5-6
EXPLORING OUR FAITH
A 4-page, 2-color Leaflet based on prayer. Includes games, illustrations, projects, classroom activities, teachings, and a family page. Please write for samples and discount schedule.

For young Catholics (grades 1-2-3)
JESUS LOVES YOU
A CATHOLIC CATECHISM FOR THE PRIMARY GRADES
A Redemptorist Pastoral Publication
Combining solid doctrine with up-to-date catechesis for the youngest Catholics, this catechism asks and answers 38 basic questions about Catholic-Christian life and belief. $4.95

Leader's Guide available — $4.95.

EXPLAINING GOD'S WORD
A 4-page Leaflet based on the Gospel reading for each Sunday. Includes games, puzzles, 2-color illustrations, plus solid, basic Catholic teaching. Please write for samples and discount schedule.

For Catholic adults
HANDBOOK FOR TODAY'S CATHOLIC
BELIEFS, PRACTICES, PRAYERS
A Redemptorist Pastoral Publication

- A mini-catechism for those who want an update on Catholic teaching
- An "answer book" for parents besieged by children's questions about God
- A review text for students of any age
- A guide for religion teachers
- An interesting, informative reference book for anyone — $1.50

Spanish edition, **MANUAL PARA EL CATOLICO DE HOY**, $1.50

The ILLUSTRATED CATECHISM
A Redemptorist Pastoral Publication
A common-sense catechism for the contemporary Catholic!

- Popular question-and-answer approach
- Over 250 illustrations
- Draws on Scripture and blends the wisdom of the past with contemporary insights into the mysteries of the Catholic faith
- 3-part pastoral supplement provides practical information needed for everyday Catholic life — $3.95

Leader's Guide available — $4.95.

ORDER FROM YOUR LOCAL BOOKSTORE
or write **Liguori Publications,** Box 060, Liguori, Missouri 63057.
(Please add 50¢ postage and handling for first
item ordered and 25¢ for each additional item.)